History Source Books

The Elizabetha

The Seamen

Peter & Mary Speed

Oxford University Press 1987

Oxford University Press, Walton Street, Oxford OX2 6DP

Oxford New York Toronto
Delhi Bombay Calcutta Madras Karachi
Petaling Jaya Singapore Hong Kong Tokyo
Nairobi Dar es Salaam Cape Town
Melbourne Auckland

and associated companies in
Beirut Berlin Ibadan Nicosia

Oxford is a trade mark of Oxford University Press

ISBN 0 19 917116 5

Typeset by Best-Set Typesetter Limited, Hong Kong
Printed in Hong Kong

Acknowledgements

The publishers would like to thank the following for permission to reproduce the photographs:

The detail from 'the Embarkation of Henry VIII' on p 48 is reproduced by gracious permission of Her Majesty the Queen. BBC Hulton Picture Library, p 75; Anne Bolt, p 17; Trustees of the British Museum, p 7; City of Plymouth Museums and Art Gallery, p 16; Crown copyright, reproduced with the permission of the Controller of Her Majesty's Stationery Office, p 65; Mary Evans Picture Library, p 12; Fotomas Index, p 42; The Hispanic Society of America, p 27; Johnson Matthey, p 33; The Master and Fellows, Magdalene College, Cambridge, pp 24, 49 top; Mansell Collection, p 39; Mas, pp 14, 18, 41, 44, 77 bottom; The National Maritime Museum, London pp 8, 15 (Weidenfeld & Nicolson Archives), 58, 61, 66, 67, 70, 77 top, 79; National Portrait Gallery, London, pp 28, 50, 76; Patrimonio Nacional/Mas, pp 56 and 57; Major D R Potts, R.A, p 45 left; Public Record Office Sp9/205/1 and Weidenfeld & Nicolson Archives, p 74; Rijksmuseum, Amsterdam, p 80; Trustees of the Science Museum, London, pp 5 top right, 49 bottom; Peter Speed, pp 4, 5 top left and bottom, 13; The Marquess of Tavistock and the Trustees of the Bedford Estates, p 72; Michael Turner, pp 2–3, 29 bottom, 60 (all with kind permission from Buckland Abbey) 20, 21, 29 top, 32, 36, 45 right; Weidenfeld & Nicolson Archives, p 55; The Worshipful Society of Apothecaries, p 68; Zefa, p 40

Illustrations by John Batchelor, Nick Hawken and Christine Molan.

Contents

1 General Introduction

In the fifteenth century, the people of Europe developed ships that could make long ocean voyages. That meant they were able to explore the world.

The Portuguese took the lead. They wanted to reach the East Indies, that were known as the Spice Islands. Spices were essential for cooking in those days, so people were willing to pay high prices for them. The Portuguese knew that if they could reach the East Indies, they would make a lot of money. They started in the middle of the fifteenth century by exploring the west coast of Africa. Then, in 1499, Vasco da Gama reached India. By the early sixteenth century, the Portuguese were bringing home not only spices, but also goods like gold and silk. They traded in huge vessels called 'carracks'. Each returned with a cargo worth, in modern money, millions of pounds.

The Spaniards tried to imitate the Portuguese. By the fifteenth century, many people were fairly sure the world was round. It seemed possible, therefore, to reach the East Indies by sailing west. One man who believed this was Christopher Columbus. He persuaded the King and Queen of Spain to give him a small fleet, and, in 1492, he crossed the Atlantic. He landed on a group of islands which we call the West Indies. Columbus was sure they were the East Indies.

Later explorers found that Columbus was wrong, and that the huge continent of America was in the way. But the Spaniards were more than satisfied with America, for they discovered rich silver mines in Mexico and Peru. Also, Spanish settlers went to the West Indies and Central America. They grew sugar cane, which was then a valuable crop.

Figure 1 Monument to the Discoveries, Lisbon This monument is in memory of the Portuguese explorers. The man in the front is Prince Henry (1394–1460). He was called the 'Navigator' because he organised many of the voyages, though he did not go to sea himself. The Portuguese erected this monument in 1960. Why did they choose that year?

Figure 2 Columbus receives his Commission This group of statues is at Cordoba, in southern Spain. It was here that King Ferdinand and Queen Isabella gave Columbus authority to go on his voyage of discovery. He is holding the document in his left hand.

In 1494 Spain and Portugal made the Treaty of Tordesillas which divided the world outside Europe between them. In 1580, Philip 11 of Spain conquered Portugal, so adding her empire to his own.

Meanwhile the English were far behind. Many of them were sailors, but their voyages did not compare with those of the Portuguese and the Spaniards. This changed during the reign of Elizabeth. English merchants went further and further afield, into the Mediterranean, into the Baltic, and even into the White Sea in the north of Russia. There were explorers, too. Francis Drake sailed round the world, the first Englishman to do so. Men like Martin Frobisher attempted to find routes to the East Indies around the north of America and the north of Asia. Some people even tried to found colonies.

Figure 3 Spanish Ship of the late Fifteenth Century It was in ships like this that Columbus and his men crossed the Atlantic. The men in the well of the ship have, of course, been drawn much too big.

However, the Elizabethan seamen are most famous for their attacks on the Spaniards and the Portuguese. These led England and Spain into war. Neither side won, but the English challenged the greatest naval power in the world and fought it to a standstill. By doing so, they became a great seafaring people themselves.

In this book, you will learn something about the exploits of the Elizabethan seamen. You will also discover what kind of men they were.

Figure 4 Plaque at Plymouth This plaque is in memory of the first English attempt to found a colony overseas. Who organised the expedition? What was the colony called? Where was it? Was it a success?

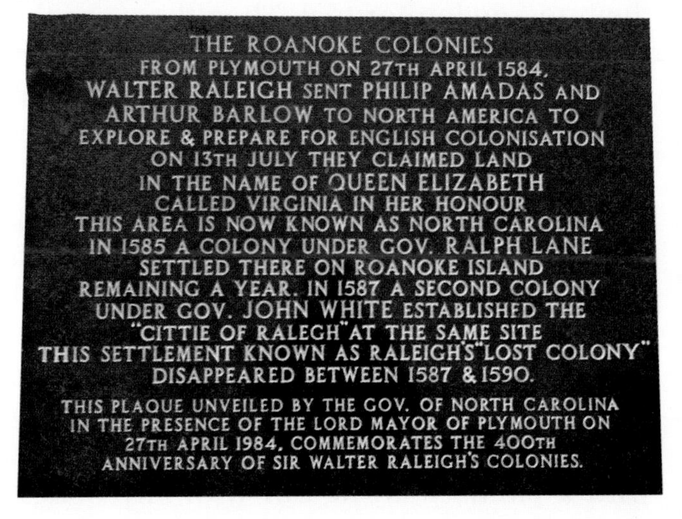

2 Pirates

A Introduction

Queen Elizabeth ruled England with the help of a group of men called the Privy Council. We will ask its Secretary, Sir Francis Walsingham, to tell us about pirates.

'Are there many pirates in England?'

'Our coasts swarm with them. They rob any ship they can find, whether it is English or foreign.'

'Who is supposed to deal with pirates?'

'The Lord Admiral.'

'Isn't his job to command the fleet?'

'Yes, but he is also responsible for law and order around our shores. Of course, he cannot do this on his own. Every seaside county has a Vice-Admiral to look after his own part of the coast.'

'Are these Vice-Admirals sailors?'

'No. They do not even have any ships. Each is chosen from the most important noblemen in his county.'

'Is there anyone to help the Vice-Admirals?'

'All Justices of the Peace should do so. Moreover, we have asked some of the Justices in each county to be Commissioners for Piracy. Their job is to arrest pirates, and send them to London for trial. Then there are the constables in charge of the Queen's castles and coastal forts. There is no shortage of men who are supposed to deal with pirates.'

'Then why do you have so many?'

'The sad truth is that nearly everyone living near the sea, makes money from pirates in one way or another. Merchants do excellent business with them. Pirates pay high prices for the supplies they need. At the same time, they sell any goods they capture, very cheaply. A merchant can do better business with a pirate, than he can with any honest trader. There are even merchants who send out pirate ships themselves. Such a man may also be a Justice of the Peace.

Figure 1 Pirates torturing a Captured Seaman

Also, pirates are clever in the way they behave. At sea, they are evil. When they capture a ship they will torture its crew, to make them say where they have hidden their money. But on shore, you would not wish for a jollier set of fellows. There is feasting and drinking, and presents for everyone. The more important the man, the better his present. Some Dorset pirates once captured a ship carrying the luggage of the Scottish ambassador in London. First of all, they took the clothes they wanted for themselves. They must have been the best dressed pirates in England. Then they gave the rest of the clothes and goods to their friends on shore. For example, the Vicar of Studland had a fine new Bible for his church, and the Mayor of Poole had a splendid pair of scarlet hose.'

Figure 2 Howard of Effingham, Lord High Admiral of England
The Admiral is shown as a soldier on horseback!

'Does the Queen have no honest men to serve her?'

'Yes, of course. She has a great many.'

'Then why not send some of them to put down the pirates and their friends?'

'It is not as easy as that. From what I have told you, you will understand that many important men make money from pirates. If the Queen annoys them, she will lose powerful friends. It looks as if we shall have a war with Spain. If we do, it is these men who must lead our armies against the Spaniards.

For example, there is Sir Richard Rogers of Blandford, in Dorset. Recently, a pirate ship was blown ashore in a gale. He rescued the stolen goods that were on her; he refloated her; he fitted her out for sea again. Meanwhile, he entertained the pirates, who, of course, paid him handsomely. We have had to call him before the Privy Council, but I am sure his punishment will be light. If there is a war, he is the only leader the men of Blandford will follow.'

'Then you are not going to stop the pirates?'

'I think we must. I was ambassador in Paris, and I know how angry the French are with our pirates. Other countries are the same. I am afraid we are drifting into war with Spain. That means we cannot allow our pirates to make enemies for us all over the rest of Europe.'

'It is a very difficult problem.'

'It is indeed. If the Queen puts down the pirates, she makes enemies at home. If she does not put them down, she makes enemies abroad.'

Note: As Sir Francis Walsingham expected, Sir Richard Rogers was not punished too severely. He was fined £100. It was a lot of money for those days, but not nearly as much as he had made from helping pirates over the years. What is more, he learnt his lesson, and became an honest man. When war broke out with Spain, it was he who drilled the men of Blandford, training them to fight any invaders that might land.

1 Who was responsible for putting down pirates?

2 Who was in charge in each of the seaside counties?

3 Who was supposed to help them?

4 Why did merchants like doing business with pirates?

5 How did pirates make sure they had plenty of friends on shore?

6 Sir Francis Walsingham said that if the Queen put down the pirates she would lose powerful friends. Why was she likely to need those friends?

7 Why was it necessary for the Queen to put down the pirates, none the less?

8 The Queen had a difficult choice to make. What was it?

9 How was the problem solved, in the case of Sir Richard Rogers?

B Activities of the Pirates

Here is a note which the Privy Council made. It tells us what certain pirates had been doing:

Document One

The *Greyhound*, laden with figs, oils etc. belonging to a Spaniard, was taken by Englishmen underneath one of the Queen's forts in the Isle of Wight. As it was within Her Majesty's protection, it will have to be restored.

Henry Knowles took and brought to the island another ship laden with sugar and spices. He daily spoils the goods, in spite of the Privy Council's orders for their delivery. Roberts of Bristol has taken two Portugal barks coming from Brazil, laden with sugars, cotton, wool, etc. The ambassador asks that the goods may be put in safe keeping till the matter be tried and such open wrongs to the King's subjects prevented.

Acts of the Privy Council, 1581

1. Where was the *Greyhound* captured?
2. Who owned her cargo?
3. What must happen to the ship?
4. What was in the ship captured by Henry Knowles?
5. What is he doing with these goods?
6. What ships did Roberts of Bristol capture?
7. What goods were they carrying?
8. What does the ambassador want done with the goods?

Figure 1 A Sixteenth Century Ship Pirates used well-armed ships like this.

In 1565 a pirate ship was wrecked in Guernsey. Some of the crew were captured and brought before the Governor of the island. Later, he wrote to the Privy Council:

Document Two

We have examined the pirates. Their chief, Captain Heidon, together with Rich, Deigle, Corbet and others, are fled. Those we have captured have confessed their faults, but plead that they were tricked by Heidon who made them pirates, pretending to go on a trading voyage to France.

Confession of Richard Hitchins, from Shackford, Devon, aged 50; Philip Redhead of Blackmore, Dorset, aged 24; Roger Shaster, apprentice to Thomas Bowes, goldsmith of London, aged 20; Robert Highgate of Oxfordshire, aged 30; and Thomas Morris of Wells, Somerset, aged 22:

They took a Flemish ship in which 13 or 14 Scots in their company sailed away, as they did not agree with the others. They committed several robberies on the coast of Spain. Having taken a wine vessel, they went to Beerhaven in Ireland, where they sold the wine. They compounded with Lord Sullivan for his help by which Heidon's and two other vessels, under Captains Corbet and Lusingham, were freed from the Queen's ships sent to take them as rovers. Lusingham, waving his cap towards the Queen's ships, was slain by a piece of ordnance. They were forced by storm into Guernsey, where the vessel perished. Heidon, Corbet, Deigle and 14 others fled in a small pinnace.

Governor of Guernsey to the Privy Council, 31 August 1566

Notes: 'compounded with Lord Sullivan'– bribed Lord Sullivan
'piece of ordnance' – cannon

1. Who was the chief of the pirates?
2. What has happened to him?
3. According to the pirates, how did he trick them? Would you believe this story?
4. How many pirates have been captured? Where in England did they come from?

Figure 2 The Death of Lusingham

5 What happened to the Flemish ship they captured?
6 Where did they do most of their robberies?
7 Why did they go to Beerhaven, in Ireland?
8 Obviously, they were captured at Beerhaven, by some of the Queen's ships. Who helped them escape?
9 How many other pirate ships escaped?
10 Who was Lusingham?
11 Why was he waving his hat at the Queen's ships, do you think?
12 What happened to him?

Later, the Governor wrote again to the Privy Council:

> *Document Three*
> We have condemned Richard Hitchins who confesses that he has been a pirate from his youth, and he has been hanged in chains. The rest, being young men, and of better hope, remain at the Queen's mercy. I should be glad to be rid of them. They are too poor to afford bail.
> *Governor of Guernsey to the Privy Council*, 20 December 1566

1 What has happened to Richard Hitchins? Why?
2 Why have the other pirates been spared, for the time being?

The Privy Council told the Governor to free the young pirates, after giving them a warning.

Here is a letter the Privy Council sent to some officials in Essex:

> *Document Four*
> We understand that Richard Basset, Vice-admiral of Essex, has sent forth a ship, under pretence of a voyage to Bordeaux. This ship has robbed certain of Her Majesty's subjects coming from the Eastern Countries. As it is supposed it will shortly return unto some port, this letter is to require you in very secret manner to lay wait upon the coast, and arrest the said ship.
> *Acts of the Privy Council*, 1581

Note: Every county along the coast had its Vice-admiral, who was the Lord Admiral's deputy. (See *Introduction*.)

1 Who is reported to have sent a pirate ship to sea?
2 Who has been robbed by these pirates?
3 What are the officials who receive this letter to do?

C The Pirates' Friends and Helpers

Pirates needed to buy food and ammunition. Also, they needed to sell the goods which they captured at sea. They found plenty of people willing to do business with them.

In 1578, a fisherman called Robert Scarborough was questioned in Yorkshire. This was what he said:

Document One

I was master of a boat whereof Thomas Thompson was captain. Coming to shore for sale of fish, we met with divers pirates, with whom Thompson spent such money as he had. We met with a fly-boat in the Humber, and bought two pieces of broad cloth, 50 pieces of pewter, and some coverings for beds. We bought near Coquet Island, three barrels of soap, 30 or 40 pieces of pewter, and seven yards of canvas, worth a shilling a yard.

Thompson and I were never pirates. But Thompson told me when we went to sea 12 months ago, that he meant to take £40 or £50 to spend with such pirates as he commonly met once a week. For this money he had of Clarke and Phippson goods worth £100, namely six bales of Holland cloth, 20 pieces of broad cloth, 200 pieces of pewter, 200 or 300 yards of canvas, and three barrels of soap.

Examination of Robert Scarborough, 25 March 1578

Notes: 'master' – second-in-command of a ship. His job was to navigate the ship.
'fly-boat' – small sailing ship

According to Robert Scarborough:

1. What goods did his captain buy from pirates?
2. What did he pay for the goods he bought from Clarke and Phippson?
3. How much were these goods worth?

Robert Scarborough also said:

Document Two

Thompson sold goods at Burlington to Consett, the Lord Admiral's deputy. Consett also bought

Figure 1 Pirate Banquet

out of other ships, whereof Nicholas White and John Gullet were captains and pirates, and victualled them at divers times.

The pirates White, Gullet and Launce were commonly victualled about Whitby by Consett and Eldrington, servants to the Lord Admiral. The pirates told me they might have victuals whether they had money or not. Having the Admiral's men for their friends, they could come on land at any place, and no man dared say anything to them. So they let the pirates have what they wanted for very little money. They continued banqueting with them for three or four days together.

The pirates also said that when they came upon the coast of Lincolnshire, they were victualled by Thorny, another servant of the Lord Admiral's. There they had what they

wanted from the Lord Admiral's men and in one night spent £30 in banqueting.
Examination of Robert Scarborough, 25 March, 1578

Notes: The Lord Admiral not only commanded the navy. He was also supposed to put down pirates.
'victuals' – supplies

According to Robert Scarborough:

1 To whom did Thompson sell some of the goods he had bought from pirates?
2 Who sold supplies to the pirates?
3 Why were the pirates able to buy supplies from other people, for very little money?
4 How did the pirates enjoy themselves with their friends?

D Recovering Goods Taken by Pirates

Sometimes the Queen's officers seized goods that had been taken by pirates. It was their duty to return these goods to their owners. In 1587, the Governor of Guernsey had some goods belonging to a French merchant. The merchant made a list of them, which he gave to one of the Governor's officials. The merchant describes what happened next:

Document One
He asked me what I meant by the title of the said list, 'Merchandizes depredées et gastées et decippées par le Sieur Gouverneur.' I answered, 'Goods made away, unloaded by night, wetted, rotted, spoiled and scattered by the Governor and his servants.' The official showed this to the Governor of Guernsey, who considered himself greatly insulted. He threatened me in a manner as was not decent for a man of his calling. He kept me in prison for three weeks and has now sent me to the Privy Council as a villain. I have lost nearly all my goods and have spent £150 these five months trying to recover them. I request a final answer, so that I may return home and spend no more time in this matter.
Petition to the Queen, August 1587

1 Explain, briefly, what the merchant accused the Governor of doing with his goods.
2 How did the Governor feel about this?
3 What did he do to the merchant?
4 How much money has the merchant spent trying to recover his goods?
5 How much time has he spent?

Here is a letter the Privy Council sent to the Town Council of Southampton:

Document Two
Complaint has been made by the Sergeant of Her Majesty's Court of the Admiralty that he, going unto the town of Southampton to recover certain goods brought there by pirates, refusal was made to assist him unless he would pay large and extraordinary fees.

There hath been a like complaint by one Adrian le Seigneur a merchant of Rouen, who having been robbed by English pirates of Brazil wood, cotton, wool, pepper and goods of great value, part whereof is brought unto that town, cannot recover the same unless he will pay intolerable fees. He had rather leave his goods than recover them on such unreasonable conditions.

We are given to understand that the exacting of so unreasonable fees grows chiefly by the inordinate disposition of one Waterton, your Town Clerk. We require you to send him to us to answer his particular doings in such matters.
Acts of the Privy Council, 1581

Note: The Sergeant of the Court of Admiralty was an important government official.

1 Why had the Sergeant of the Court of Admiralty gone to Southampton?
2 What was he told when he arrived?
3 What goods did the French merchant lose?
4 What was he told?
5 Who has been making these unreasonable demands?
6 What must the Town Council do with him?

E Measures Against Pirates

Many foreigners complained about the English pirates. It looked as if England was going to lose all her friends abroad. Accordingly, the Queen ordered her officials in the seaside counties to do everything they could to put down pirates. By no means all of them obeyed, but some did. Here is part of a letter the Privy Council wrote to the Vice-Admiral of Dorset:

Document One
There have been arrested within the Bay of Studland in the county of Dorset, one John Pierce, a very notorious pirate, with 15 of his crew. You are to proceed to their trial and so to their execution according to law. And it is desired that some of the pirates may be executed at Studland to the terrifying of others, for that same place hath been much frequented with pirates. Upon their condemnation some of the pirates are to be hanged at certain gibbets to be erected thereabouts.
Acts of the Privy Council, 1581

1 How many pirates have been arrested?
2 What is the name of their leader?

Figure 1 A Hanging

3 Where are some of the pirates to be executed? Why?

The Privy Council also wrote to the Vice-Admiral of Cornwall:

Document Two
There is lately arrested at Studland in the county of Dorset, one John Pierce, a very notorious pirate, who has an old mother dwelling at Padstow, noted to be a witch, to whom, it is reported, the said Pierce has conveyed all such goods and spoils as he has wickedly gotten at sea. We desire your Lordship to give orders for the examination of the said Pierce's mother to discover whether she be a witch indeed, and what spoils and goods she has received from her son.
Acts of the Privy Council, 1581

1 Where does John Pierce's mother live?
2 What is she thought to be?
3 What might Pierce have been giving her?
4 What two things must the Vice-Admiral discover?

Later in 1581, the Privy Council had a letter from the Vice-Admiral of Dorset. This is how it replied:

Document Three
We have your letter telling of the escape of Pierce and Walsh the pirates out of the gaol of Dorchester by the bribing of the keeper, and the taking of them again by Mr. Henry Howard, your Lordship's son. We have called the said Mr. Henry Howard before us to thank him, and give him encouragement to persist in that good course, whereof we intend to inform Her Majesty, to his further comfort.
Acts of the Privy Council, 1581

1 How did the pirates escape from Dorchester gaol?
2 Who recaptured them?
3 How is he being rewarded?

Pierce and some of his crew were hanged at Studland as the Privy Council had ordered. The gibbets were erected at the low water mark, so that when the sea came in, it

Figure 2 Studland Bay today

washed over the corpses. That night, some pirates in Studland Bay crept ashore, cut down the gibbets, and took away Pierce's body.

It was unusual for Henry Howard to be in the Privy Council's good books. He was in trouble with it several times. Once was for ill-treating his wife, and once for assaulting the High Sheriff of Dorset. On another occasion he had a cart load of pirates' loot delivered to his father's house, Bindon Abbey.

The government sometimes had help from men who were even more dishonest then Henry Howard. In 1577, a particularly wicked pirate called John Callice was captured. He was condemned to death, so, trying to save his life, he wrote this letter to Sir Francis Walsingham one of the Queen's ministers:

Document Four
I bewail my former wicked life and beseech God and Her Majesty to forgive me. If she will spare my life, I will serve her by sea, with those she can best trust, to clear the coasts of other wicked pirates. I know their haunts, roads, creeks, and maintainers so well, I can do more than if she sent ships and spent £20,000. I send herewith the names of my fellow pirates and the maintainers and victuallers of me and my companions.
Letter to Sir Francis Walsingham, 1577

1. What does Callice offer to do, in return for his life?
2. Why will his help be very valuable?
3. What information does he send with his letter?

The Privy Council accepted Callice's offer of help, and he was pardoned. What did the people he betrayed think of him, do you suppose?

In the end, the government sent ships to round up the pirates at sea. A good many were caught and hanged. Most of the others were so frightened that they changed their ways. Some, however, could not live without excitement. Their chance came when war broke out between England and Spain. Elizabeth's government allowed them to attack Spanish ships, Spanish colonies and even Spain itself.

3 John Hawkins's Voyage to the West Indies, 1567–1568

A Introduction

By the middle of the sixteenth century there were, as you already know, many Spanish settlers in the West Indies and Central America. They were farmers, whose main crop was sugar cane. Growing sugar cane was very hard work. It killed many of the local Indians whom the Spaniards used as slaves. As a result, the settlers badly needed the much stronger negro slaves that could be brought from West Africa. However, the Spanish government made life difficult for the settlers. It forbade them to trade with any merchants but Spaniards. At the same time, it put such high taxes on slaves, that few Spanish merchants would deal in them. The settlers were desperate for someone to bring them slaves, and buy their sugar. Since Spanish merchants would not do this, many settlers were willing to break the law and trade with other Europeans. The French and the English soon realised they could make a lot of money, selling slaves in the Spanish colonies.

The first Englishman to take part in the slave trade was John Hawkins. He made a voyage in 1563, and another in 1565. In 1567, he sailed on a third voyage. He took with him six ships. Four were his own. One of them, the *Judith*, was commanded by a young relative. His name was Francis Drake. The two most important ships in the fleet belonged to Queen Elizabeth. They were the *Jesus of Lubeck* and the *Minion*. The Queen lent Hawkins these ships because she wanted a share in the profits from the voyage. At the same time, she was anxious not to upset King Philip of Spain. She gave Hawkins strict instructions to keep out of trouble with the Spaniards.

Hawkins knew it would be difficult to obey the Queen. The Spanish settlers might welcome him, but the Spanish officials who worked for the King would not. How would you feel if someone forced his way into your house and, without your permission, opened a shop in your front room? That is what the Spanish government thought about Hawkins.

Figure 1 A Spaniard with American Indian Slave The Spaniards worked many Indians to death.

1 What crop did the Spanish settlers grow?
2 What slaves did the settlers need to cultivate it?
3 Why were Spanish merchants unwilling to supply these slaves?
4 Who was the first Englishman to take part in the slave trade?
5 When did he leave on his third voyage?
6 How many ships did he have? Who commanded one of them?
7 Why did Queen Elizabeth lend two ships?
8 What instructions did she give?
9 Why were these instructions difficult to obey?

B Hawkins in West Africa

Hawkins left Plymouth on October 2nd. 1567. He arrived off Cape Verde, in West Africa, in the middle of November. Job Hortop, a gunner on the *Jesus of Lubeck*, describes an adventure there:

Document One
In the river in the night time we had one of our pinnaces capsized by a sea-horse, so that our men were swimming about in the river. They were all taken into the other pinnaces, except two that were carried away by the seahorse. This monster is the size of a horse, saving that his legs be short, and his teeth very great and a span in length. At night he goes into the woods, seeking to devour the negroes in their cabins. The negroes keep watch, and when they are gone into the woods, they lay a great tree across the way. On their return, for that their legs be so short, they cannot go over it. Then the negroes set upon them with their bows, arrows and darts, and so destroy them.
The Travels of Job Hortop

1 What animal might Hortop be describing?
2 How do the negroes capture it?

But Hawkins and his men had not come to Africa to study natural history. They wanted to collect slaves. Hortop says what happened at their first attempt:

Document Two
Our General was the first that leapt on land. There we took certain negroes, but not without damage to ourselves. For our General, Captain Dudley and eight others of our company were hurt with poisoned arrows. About nine days after, eight that were wounded died. Our General was taught by a negro to draw the poison out of his wound with a clove of garlic, whereby he was cured.
The Travels of Job Hortop

Note: 'our general' – John Hawkins

1 What did the negroes fire at the English?
2 How many of the English died?
3 Who saved Hawkins? How?

Figure 2 West African Natives

Hawkins and his men only managed to capture a few negroes. It looked as if their voyage was going to be a failure. But then they had a piece of luck. Hawkins wrote:

Document Three
There came to us a negro, sent from a king, at war with other kings, asking for our help. He promised us that as many negroes as might be captured in these wars, should be ours. We decided to give him aid. I went myself, and with the help of the king of our side, attacked the enemy town both by land and sea. We set fire to it and put the inhabitants to flight, where we took 250 persons, men, women and children. Our friend the king took 600 persons, whereof we hoped to have had our choice. But the negro king stole away that night with his prisoners, so that we had to be content with those we had taken ourselves.
The Third Troublesome Voyage by Mr. John Hawkins

1 Why did the negro king ask Hawkins for help?
2 What did he promise Hawkins in return?
3 How many prisoners did Hawkins's men capture?
4 How many prisoners did the negro king capture?
5 What did he do, during the night?

In spite of this disappointment, Hawkins now had about 450 slaves. It was enough to make the voyage across the Atlantic worth while.

C Hawkins at Rio de la Hacha

Hawkins had been joined by a Frenchman, Captain Bland, and he had captured some Portuguese ships. He now had ten vessels in all. This powerful fleet left West Africa on February 3rd 1568, and arrived in the West Indies on March 27th. Hawkins then began selling his slaves to Spaniards living on the coast of South America. He had few problems until he arrived at a town called Rio de la Hacha. The governor there was Miguel de Castellanos. Later, in a report to the King of Spain, he described what happened:

Document One

On June 10th. of this year, John Hawkins, English corsair, arrived off the port of this city. He came in command of ten very handsome ships.

Figure 1 John Hawkins This portrait was painted when Hawkins was 58. When he was at Rio de la Hacha, he was only 35.

As soon as he had arrived, he sent me a letter in which he offered me great gifts if I would permit him to trade; and if I would not, he made great threats. I answered what your majesty has ordered, that I would by no means yield a single point. After much argument he landed his forces three quarters of a league down the coast. I then manned a fort which is built on the road by which he must advance, and there resisted him as fully as I was able. I inflicted serious damage on him, but because of his superior numbers, could not prevent him from taking the fort. When he had taken the fort, he also took the town.

Miguel de Castellanos to the Crown, 26 September 1568

According to Castellanos:

1 What did Hawkins demand?
2 How did Castellanos reply?
3 Where did Hawkins land?
4 Where did Castellanos try to stop Hawkins from reaching the town?
5 Why did he fail?

Two Spanish officials in Rio de la Hacha also wrote to the King of Spain. They said this about Castellanos:

Document Two

He went out to meet the English with 60 men, and with this, the small force that he had, he offered as fine and brave a defence as has ever been made in these Indies. He killed more than 30 of the enemy. All were astonished at his great valour, for certainly it was a business that today, looking back at it, fills with fright those who were present.

In good order he withdrew with this small force, without losing a man, whereas truly it seemed incredible that any should have escaped.

Adrete and Castillo to the Crown, 26 September, 1568

According to Adrete and Castillo:

1 How well did Castellanos resist the English?
2 How many English were killed?
3 How many Spaniards were killed?

Figure 2 Cutting Sugar Cane The Spaniards badly needed negro slaves to do hard work like this.

Castellanos also said in his report to the King:

Document Three

When Hawkins had taken the town, he sent to me again, asking me to permit trade. He said that unless I did so, he would burn and destroy the town and invade the interior and capture and steal whatever he might find. I told him to do as he pleased, since I preferred to lose my worldly goods rather than disobey your majesty's commands. At once, he began to fire the town, and that day he burnt about one half of it.

That night a negro and a mulatto, slaves of mine, deserted to the enemy and told him they would lead him to the place where I had buried your majesty's treasure chest. That night they fell on a tent where I had all my goods and where some poor and sick people and some women were in hiding. They threatened them that unless they were ransomed they would be killed. In order that such terrible cruelty might not be carried out, for 4000 pesos of gold, I ransomed them, on condition that they delivered to me the mulatto and the negro aforesaid. I paid the 4000 pesos and the enemy released the prisoners. They delivered to me the mulatto and the negro and I handed them over to your majesty's royal law that they might be punished and made an example to all the rest on this coast. The mulatto was hung and the negro was quartered.

Miguel de Castellanos to the Crown, 26 September 1568

Note: 'mulatto' – someone who has one white parent, and one black parent

According to Castellanos:

1 What did Hawkins demand when he had taken the town?
2 What was Castellanos's answer?
3 What did Hawkins do when he received this answer?
4 What did the mulatto and the negro do for Hawkins?
5 What people did Hawkins capture?
6 How did Castellanos save them?
7 What did Hawkins agree to do with the mulatto and the negro?
8 What happened to them, in the end?

Here now, is John Hawkins's account of what happened at Rio de la Hacha:

Document Four

The governor would not agree to any trade or allow us to take water. He had fortified the town with bulwarks and obtained a hundred harquebuses. He thought by famine to have made us put on land our negroes. This would have happened, unless we entered the town by force. With 200 men we broke through their bulwarks and entered the town with the loss of only two men. There was no hurt done to the Spaniards, because after they had fired a volley, they all fled.

Thus having the town, as partly by the Spaniards' desire of negroes, and partly by the friendship of the governor, we had a secret trade. The Spaniards came to us by night, and bought of us 200 negroes.

The Third Troublesome Voyage by Mr. John Hawkins

Notes: 'bulwarks' – earth walls
'harquebuses' – muskets

According to Hawkins:

1 What did the governor forbid the English to do?
2 What had he done to defend the town?
3 What did he think hunger would compel the English to do?
4 With how many men did Hawkins attack? What did he succeed in doing?
5 How many of the English were killed?
6 Why was none of the Spaniards hurt?
7 Why were the English able to sell slaves to the Spaniards?
8 When did this trade take place?
9 How many slaves did the English sell?

Figure 3 Spanish Settlement in the West Indies. We have no picture of Rio de la Hacha, but it would have been very like this.

Later, the master of the *Jesus of Lubeck*, Robert Barrett, was captured by the Spaniards. This is what he told them happened after Hawkins had taken Rio de la Hacha:

Document Five

The governor had a meeting with Hawkins. He offered him 4000 pesos from the king's chest, if he would leave the town and go, and another 1000 pesos of his own, if, for those 1000 pesos, Hawkins would give him twenty slaves. On these terms they came to an agreement and made peace. Hawkins then did business with the citizens. He sold them 150 negroes and cloth and linens in exchange for gold, pearls and silver. He sent the governor sixty negroes in exchange for the 4000 pesos which had been given him from the king's chest.

I saw Hawkins and the governor exchange presents. Hawkins gave the governor a velvet cloak with gold buttons and pearls, and a gown lined with fur. The governor gave Hawkins a woman's girdle of large pearls, a very rich thing.

Statement of Robert Barrett, 8 October 1568

According to Barrett:

1 What did Hawkins agree to do in return for 4000 pesos belonging to the King of Spain?
2 What did Hawkins give the governor, in return for 1000 pesos?
3 How many slaves did Hawkins sell to the citizens of Rio de la Hacha?
4 What did they give him in exchange?
5 Why did Hawkins send Castellanos 60 slaves?
6 What presents did Hawkins and Castellanos give each other?

Figure 4 Englishman offering Slaves for Sale

As you can see, it is not easy to decide what really happened at Rio de la Hacha. The Spaniards tell their King that they wanted nothing to do with Hawkins, and did their best to resist him. The English say that, after a short fight, the Spaniards traded willingly, and that the governor and Hawkins even became friends. How can we discover the truth?

You will have met this kind of problem in your own daily life. Suppose a teacher comes upon two boys who are fighting, and there are no witnesses. How can the teacher find out what happened? Usually, his best plan is to question each boy on his own. Where both boys say the same thing, he can be reasonably sure he has the truth. Where they say different things, he cannot be sure at all. He must use his judgement, and try to decide which story is the more likely to be true.

Similarly, we will ask questions about the events at Rio de la Hacha. Next, we will look for the answers in the documents. Finally, we will use our judgement, to decide whether the answers are true.

Here are some questions you might ask. Probably, you can think of others:

1. Did Hawkins come to Rio de la Hacha to sell slaves?
2. Did the governor, at first, refuse him permission?
3. Did Hawkins's men take the town?
4. How many Spaniards were killed in the fight?
5. Did the Spaniards resist bravely?
6. How many English were killed?
7. Did a mulatto and a negro help Hawkins?
8. Did Hawkins betray them, by returning them to the Spaniards?
9. Did Hawkins sell slaves to the Spaniards?
10. Did Hawkins and the governor exchange gifts?

You will be able to discover the true answers to some of these questions quite easily. With others, you must use your judgement. For example, the answer to question 4 may help you with your answer to question 5. Also, Hawkins says nothing about betraying a mulatto and a negro. But would he be likely to tell this story himself? Again, the Spaniards say nothing about trading with the English. But would they have admitted to their King that they had done so?

When you have decided on the answers to all the questions you want to ask, write your own story of what happened at Rio de la Hacha. Make your story as true as you can.

D Hawkins arrives at San Juan de Ulua

By the time they left Rio de la Hacha, the English had sold nearly all their slaves. Also, the hurricane season was near. Hawkins decided to leave for home. Unfortunately, there was a violent storm which badly damaged the *Jesus*. At the time, the fleet was near the coast of Mexico, and there was only one harbour in which to take refuge. This was San Juan de Ulua. Hawkins had no choice but go there.

San Juan de Ulua was just a small island, about a quarter of a mile across, and half a mile from the mainland. It had a quay where ships could tie up, a fort, and a few buildings, but that was all. However, the place was important for two reasons. One was that it lay opposite the town of Vera Cruz, from where the road led to Mexico City, the capital of New Spain. The second reason was that it was the only port on the coast that would shelter ships from the violent north winds. These were certain to sink any vessel that they caught in the open sea.

Hawkins arrived at San Juan de Ulua on Thursday, August 16th. 1568. The Spaniards there were not strong enough to resist him. He took over the fort and placed in it eleven guns from his ships. The very next day, a fleet of thirteen Spanish ships appeared. The admiral of these ships was Juan de Ubilla. There were some soldiers on board, commanded by Francisco de Luxan. Moreover, travelling with the fleet was the most important Spaniard in America. He was the Viceroy of New Spain, Don Martin Enriquez. It was Enriquez who now took charge.

The Spanish fleet gave Hawkins a problem. Later, he wrote:

Document One
'Now', said I, 'I am in two dangers and forced to receive one of them'. That was, either I must keep the fleet from entering the Port, or else allow them to enter in with their treason, which they never fail to use, when they have the chance. If I had kept them out there would have been a shipwreck of all the fleet, which amounted in value to £1,800,000. This I considered I was not able to answer, fearing the Queen's anger in so weighty a matter.
The Third Troublesome Voyage by Mr. John Hawkins

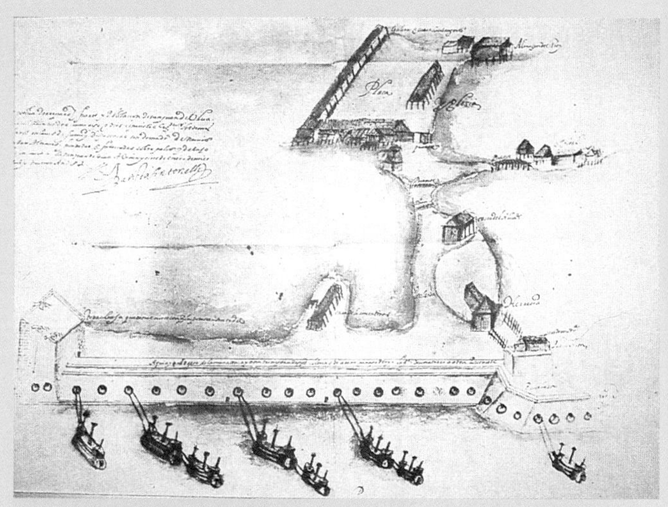

Figure 1 San Juan de Ulua in the Sixteenth Century and (right) **Figure 2**, Suan Juan de Ulua Today. The rings used to moor the ships are still there.

Note: By 'treason', Hawkins meant treachery. He felt the Spaniards were not to be trusted.

1. What was Hawkins afraid the Spaniards would do if he allowed them into the port, do you suppose?
2. What was Hawkins afraid would happen to the Spanish fleet, if he kept it out of the port?
3. Why would this annoy Queen Elizabeth? (See *Introduction*.)

In the end, Hawkins allowed the Spaniards to enter the port. He wrote:

Document Two
I thought it rather better to run the risk of their treason. This, by good policy, I hoped might be prevented, so I sent them my conditions. I said there should be twelve gentlemen given as hostages by both sides; and that the Island should be in our possession during our stay there, along with such guns as were planted there; and that no Spaniard might land in the Island with any kind of weapon.
The Third Troublesome Voyage by Mr. John Hawkins

1 On what conditions did Hawkins say he would allow the Spanish fleet to enter the port?

While Hawkins was wondering what to do, so also were the Spaniards. Later, Don Martin Enriquez said:

Document Three
I called a council aboard the flagship, summoning General Francisco de Luxan and all the captains and masters of the ships of the fleet. I asked them to say whether or not it would be well to force an entrance to the harbour. They said it was not wise to enter by force, but peacefully to make the port and tie up the ships. Until this was done, the ships were in danger of loss, for the wind was from the north. Also, the enemy had the advantage, in that he was in the harbour. In view of this opinion, I decided to enter on terms of peace, until my ships should be tied up in the harbour.
Statement of Don Martin Enriquez, 27 September 1568

1 What advice was Enriquez given by his officers?
2 In view of that advice, what did Enriquez decide to do?

Document Four is the letter which Enriquez sent to Hawkins:

Document Four
I well believe that your honour's arrival in this port was forced by the great need your honour had of food and other things. So also I am certain that, as your honour says, your honour has not ill-treated any subject of his majesty's. Nor has your fleet done any damage at the ports where it has called, but that your honour has done nothing but trade in slaves and other goods. Therefore, I am content to accept the proposal which your honour makes in your letter, asking me to deliver hostages, and to enter the port in peace. And I am very confident than when we meet, friendship will grow between these fleets, since both are so well disciplined.
Enriquez to Hawkins, 18 September 1568

1 Judging from Enriquez's letter:
  a What reason did Hawkins give for being in San Juan de Ulua?
  b How had he been treating the Spaniards he had met on his voyage, did he say? Was this true?
2 What does Enriquez agree to do?
3 What does he say will happen when the two fleets are together?

When the agreement had been made, the Spaniards entered the port. They arrived, as Hawkins said, 'the two fleets saluting one another as the manner of the sea doth require.'

E The Battle at San Juan de Ulua

As soon as they were safely in harbour, the Spaniards made plans to capture the English. Enriquez said:

Document One

I decided the attack should be made as follows. A cargo ship, with 150 men hidden on board, should be brought up between the Spanish and English flagships; and that General Luxan and Admiral de Ubilla should go with this party and try to come alongside the English flagship.

And when they had arrived near enough to board, General Luxan should make a sign to me and I, from my flagship, would order a trumpet to be blown. At this signal, Captain Antonio Delgadillo with men from Vera Cruz, and Captain Pedro de Yebra, with men from the same town, should attack the island. They were to take the forts and the guns which the English had in them.

Statement of Don Martin Enriquez, 27 September 1568.

Figure 1 The battle at San Juan de Ulua

1. How many men were to be hidden on the cargo ship?
2. Which officers were to go with them?
3. Where was the cargo ship to go?
4. What was General Luxan to do when it arrived?
5. What would Enriquez do then?
6. What were the men from Vera Cruz to do?

According to Enriquez, this was what, in fact, happened:

Document Two

An hour before the time set, and when the cargo ship was still far distant from the English flagship, and having no order to do so, Admiral Juan de Ubilla gave the sign it was General Luxan's duty to make. At this, I thought all was ready, and had the trumpet blown. At this signal, Captains Delgadillo and de Yebra attacked the island. They took the forts, putting to flight the English who were there. With the guns taken from them, they bombarded the enemy's fleet.

But because Juan de Ubilla made the sign so far ahead of time, the party in the cargo ship was unable to board the English flagship. The enemy were able to open fire with their guns and escape with their flagship and a shallop. They left behind their admiral and four other vessels.

Statement of Don Martin Enriquez, 27 September 1568

Notes: By the English flagship the Spaniards meant the *Minion*, the admiral was the *Jesus of Lubeck* and the shallop was Drake's little ship, the *Judith*.

1. Who gave the signal from the cargo ship?
2. According to Enriquez, why was this a mistake?
3. What did Enriquez do, when he saw the signal?

4 Who took the island? What did they do with the guns there?
5 What were the men in the cargo ship unable to do? Why?
6 Which English ships escaped?
7 How many English ships did the Spaniards capture?

Most of the Spaniards thought that if de Ubilla had not given the signal too soon, all the English ships would have been taken. He was asked to explain why he had done so. Here is his answer:

Document Three
Once aboard the cargo ship, I ordered the men to join me and haul away at the bows in order to grapple with the English flagship. But the English recognised me and suspected what was happening. The English captain told me I was not behaving like a gentlemen, and had tricked them. I said I was behaving like a captain and a fighter. The English captain said I was quite right and fired an arrow at me. At the same time, his companion fired a musket which killed a soldier at my side. I went to speak to General Luxan, but I could not find him. And so I made the signal to our flagship. The trumpet sounded, and we cried 'Santiago!' The enemy attacked us, and we attacked them. We tried to come alongside them, but haul as we would, they moved off faster and got away.
Statement of Juan de Ubilla, 29 September 1568

1 What excuse did Juan de Ubilla give for making the signal too soon? Explain briefly, in your own words.
2 Do you think de Ubilla's excuse was a good one?

We must now look at some English accounts of the battle. Hawkins said he became suspicious on the morning of the attack, for the Spaniards were busy moving men and weapons. He went on:

Document Four
We suspected a great number of men to be hid in a great cargo ship which was moored next unto the *Minion*. Robert Barrett, the master of the *Jesus*, who could speak Spanish, I sent to the Viceroy to ask if it was true. The Viceroy, seeing that his treachery must be discovered, arrested our master and blew a trumpet. The Spaniards then set upon us from all sides.

Our men who were on shore were stricken with a sudden fear. They tried to flee to the ships. The Spaniards landed in multitudes and slew all our men on shore without mercy. A few of them escaped on board the *Jesus*. The great cargo ship which had, I estimate, 300 men placed in her secretly, at once fell aboard the *Minion*.
The Third Troublesome Voyage by Mr. John Hawkins

Note: 'master' – ship's pilot. He was second-in-command, after the captain.

1 According to Hawkins, where was the cargo ship?
2 What did he suspect about her?
3 Whom did he send to the Viceroy, to find out if this was true?
4 What did the Viceroy do when the man arrived?
5 What happened on shore?
6 What did the Spaniards in the cargo ship do?

Job Hortop describes the fighting between the English and the Spaniards in the cargo ship:

Document Five
The faithless Spaniards sounded a trumpet and therewith 300 of them entered the *Minion*. At this our General, with a loud, firm voice called unto us, saying, 'God and St. George, upon these traiterous villains, and rescue the *Minion*. I trust in God that the day shall be ours.' With that, the sailors and soldiers leapt out of the *Jesus* and into the *Minion* and beat out the Spaniards.
The Travels of Job Hortop

According to Hortop:

1 How many Spaniards boarded the *Minion*?
2 How was the ship recaptured?

Figure 2 The *Jesus of Lubeck*

Each English ship was moored with two cables. One tied its bows to the jetty. The other tied its stern to an anchor that had been dropped well out to sea. The sailors cut the bow cables. They then hauled their ships away from the jetty by pulling on the stern cables. Hawkins describes what happened next:

Document Six

Now when the *Jesus* and the *Minion* were gotten about two ships length from the Spanish fleet, the fight began hot on all sides. Within one hour the Admiral of the Spaniards was thought sunk, their Vice-admiral burned and one other of their biggest ships thought sunk, so that their ships were little able to annoy us. But all the guns on the island were in the Spaniards' hands. They cut all the masts and yards of the *Jesus*, so that there was no hope to carry her away. Also, they sunk our small ships. Whereupon we decided to place the *Jesus* between the *Minion* and the battery on land, to protect her from the guns. When it was night, we would take as much from the *Jesus* as the time would allow, and so leave her.

The Third Troublesome Voyage by Mr. John Hawkins

Note: Admiral and Vice-admiral here means the ships commanded by those men.

1 How many Spanish ships did Hawkins think were destroyed?
2 Why could Hawkins not be sure whether a Spanish ship was sunk, do you suppose? (Remember the Spaniards were near the shore.)
3 Which guns did most harm to the English?
4 Which English ship was badly damaged? Which English ships were sunk?
5 How did Hawkins protect the *Minion*?

Job Hortop describes an incident during the battle:

Document Seven
Our General bravely cheered up his soldiers and gunners, and called to Samuel his page for a cup of beer, who brought it to him in a silver cup. He, drinking to all men, told the gunners to stand to their guns like men. He had no sooner put the cup down, but a cannon ball hit it, and ran out the other side of the ship. This nothing dismayed our General, for he ceased not to encourage us, saying, 'Fear nothing, for God who has saved me from this shot will also deliver us from these traitors and villains.'
The Travels of Job Hortop

Hawkins describes how the battle ended. You will remember that the crippled *Jesus* was lying close to the *Minion*:

Document Eight
Suddenly, the Spaniards set fire to two great ships, which were coming directly towards us. Having no means to avoid the fire, it bred among our men a marvellous fear. The *Minion's* men, without either consent of the Captain or Master, sailed off, so that very hardly I was received into the *Minion*.

The most part of the men that were left alive in the *Jesus* followed the *Minion* in a small boat. The rest which the little boat was not able to take, were left at the mercy of the Spaniards.

So with the *Minion* only and the *Judith* (a small bark of 50 tons) we escaped. The same bark that night forsook us in our great misery.
The Third Troublesome Voyage by Mr. John Hawkins

Note: 'very hardly I was received into the *Minion'* – I only just managed to jump into the *Minion*.

1 What made the English sailors panic?
2 What did the crew of the *Minion* do?
3 How did some of the crew of the *Jesus* escape?
4 What happened to the rest?
5 Which was the only ship to escape with the *Minion*?
6 What did that ship do in the night?

We have, then, Spanish and English accounts of what happened at San Juan de Ulua. To try and discover the truth we must first ask questions. Here are a few, though you could certainly think of some more:

1 Did the Spaniards decide to break their word and attack the English?
2 What was the signal for the attack?
3 Did the Spaniards capture the island?
4 What did they do with the guns there?
5 Did the Spaniards try to board the *Minion* from a cargo ship?
6 Did they manage to board her, only to be driven off?
7 How many Spanish ships were destroyed?
8 How many English ships were destroyed? How many escaped?

Look for your answers in both the Spanish and the English documents. Most of the questions should give you no trouble at all, because the Spaniards and the English agree. Question 6 is difficult, though, because the Spaniards and the English say different things. Can you decide between them?

Can you be at all sure about the answer to Question 7?

How do you think the Spaniards behaved? Most Englishmen alive at the time, thought they were traitors. You may agree, but you should try to see the Spanish point of view. Imagine you are Don Martin Enriquez. Write a letter defending your actions.

F After the Battle

Job Hortop describes what happened after the battle:

Document One
We set sail, seeking the river of Panuco for water, of which we had very little. Victuals were so scarce that we were driven to eat hides, cats, rats, parrots, monkeys and dogs. Our General was forced to divide his company into two parts, for there was a mutiny among them for want of victuals. Some said they had rather be on the shore to shift for themselves among enemies, than to starve on ship-board. He asked them who would go on shore and who would tarry on ship-board. Those that would go on shore he willed to go the foremast, and those that would remain, to the baft mast. Fourscore and sixteen of us were willing to depart. Our General gave unto every one of us six yards of cloth, and money. When we were landed, he came unto us. He embraced every one of us, saying he was greatly grieved that he was forced to leave us behind. He advised us to serve God and to love one another. Then he gave us a sorrowful farewell. He promised, if God sent him safe home, he would do what he could, that so many of us as lived should by some means be brought to England.

Since my return to England, I have heard that many disliked that he left us behind and brought away negroes. But the reason is this; for them he might have had victuals, or any other thing needful, if by foul weather he had been driven upon the Islands.
The Travels of Job Hortop

According to Job Hortop:

1 What were the sailors on the *Minion* forced to eat?
2 Why did some of them want to be put on shore?
3 How many agreed to leave the ship?
4 What did Hawkins give to each of them?
5 How did Hawkins seem to feel about leaving the men?
6 What did he promise to do for them?
7 Why did Hawkins put sailors ashore, while he kept negroes on the ship?

Another sailor, Miles Philips, tells a different story of the way the men were put ashore. He says, as Hortop does, that many asked to leave the ship, but goes on:

Document Two
When our General resolved to set half his people ashore, it was amazing to see how suddenly men's minds were altered. They who a little before wanted to be set on land, were now of another mind, and asked rather to stay. It would have caused any stony heart to melt to hear the pitiful moan that many did make. The weather was stormy and therefore we were to be rowed ashore with great danger. But there was nothing for it. We that were chosen to go away, must do so. Howbeit, those that went in the first boat were safely set on shore. But of them that went in the second, of which I was one, the seas were so high that we could not reach the shore. And therefore we were made by the cruel dealing of John Hampton, captain of the *Minion*, to leap out of the boat into the main sea. We were more than a mile from the shore, and had to shift for ourselves, either to sink or swim. And of those that were made to leap into the sea, there were two drowned.
A Discourse by one Miles Philips

According to Miles Philips:

1 How did the men feel about being put ashore, when the time came to leave?
2 Why was it dangerous to leave the ship?
3 What happened to the first boat load of men?
4 What happened to the second boat load of men?

Here again, we have two accounts of the same thing. Whose story do you believe, Hortop's or Philips's?

Five months after the battle at San Juan de Ulua, Drake arrived at Plymouth with the *Judith*. A few days later, Hawkins reached Mounts Bay in Cornwall with the *Minion*. Six

Figure 1 Spanish Mine Miles Philips was overseer in a place like this.

ships had set out, carrying 400 men. Two ships and 70 men returned. As for the sailors that Hawkins set ashore, very few of them found their way back to England. You will have guessed that Job Hortop and Miles Philips did so, because you have read documents written by them. Both had remarkable adventures, especially Miles Philips.

After they had landed, Miles Philips and his companions struggled through the jungle for several days. They suffered from hunger and thirst, and they were attacked by Indians. They were pleased when they were captured by the Spaniards. The Spaniards took them to Mexico City where they were offered to anyone who wanted them as servants. Miles Philips was lucky, because he found a master who sent him to work in a silver mine. Here, he supervised the negro slaves and made himself a lot of money.

All went well for six years, when some judges of the Spanish Inquisition arrived in Mexico. They ordered that every Englishman should be arrested, and tried. Three were burnt to death, and many others were flogged. Again, Miles Philips was lucky, since he had only to be a servant in a monastery for four years. At the end of that time, he worked for a weaver and, again, managed to make some money. By now many of his companions had found themselves wives, and had settled down in Mexico. Miles, however, was determined to return to England, if he could. He was forbidden to leave Mexico City, but he ran away and went to San Juan de Ulua. By now he could speak perfect Spanish, and, after several narrow escapes, he met a ship's captain who was willing to take him to Spain. Here, he had still more adventures, until he found an English ship which brought him home. He had been away for sixteen years.

4 Francis Drake's Expedition to the Isthmus of Panama, 1572–1573

A Introduction

Drake led expeditions to the West Indies in 1570 and 1571. He attacked Spanish ships and settlements, and he learnt a lot about the coast of the Isthmus of Panama. For one thing, he found an excellent natural harbour, a safe distance from the Spaniards. He called it Port Pheasant. It was just the place to repair ships, take on water, and hunt game for fresh meat.

Then, in 1572, Drake decided to try something really ambitious. This was to capture some Spanish treasure while it was still on the mainland.

Figure 1 Francis Drake

The map shows the route the treasure followed. First of all, ships brought it along the coast of South America to Panama. Next, trains of mules carried it over the Isthmus of Panama to Nombre de Dios. From here, a powerful fleet, or 'flota', took it to Spain. Drake thought it would be a good idea to capture Nombre de Dios and rob the treasure houses there. This might have been a sound plan, but there was one thing seriously wrong with it. Drake did not leave England until May and by then the flota, with all the treasure, had arrived safely in Spain. As the flota sailed at about the same time every year, Drake should have known this was likely.

Drake had 73 men and two ships, the *Pascha* of 70 tons, and the *Swan* of 25 tons. He also had three pinnaces, which were large rowing boats. They were better than sailing ships for making surprise attacks, since they were faster. Also, they could be driven right on to beaches so that men could land. For the Atlantic crossing they were taken to pieces and carried on the ships.

1. What did Drake learn on his voyages of 1570 and 1571?
2. What harbour did he discover?
3. What did Drake decide to try in 1572?
4. What town did he want to capture? Why?
5. What was wrong with Drake's plan?
6. How many men did Drake have?
7. How many ships did he have?
8. What were pinnaces?
9. When were they more useful than sailing ships? Why?
10. How were they carried across the Atlantic?

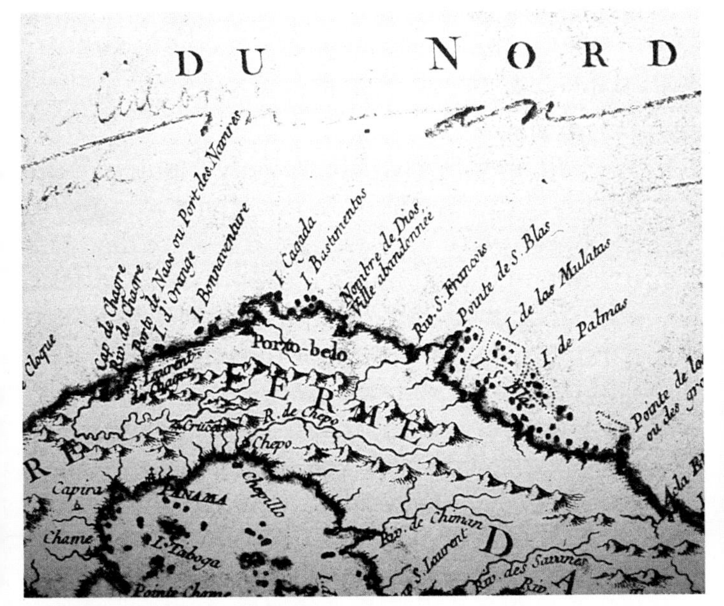

Figure 2 Isthmus of Panama

Figure 3 Scenery in the Isthmus of Panama

Figure 4 Title Page of *Sir Francis Drake Revived*

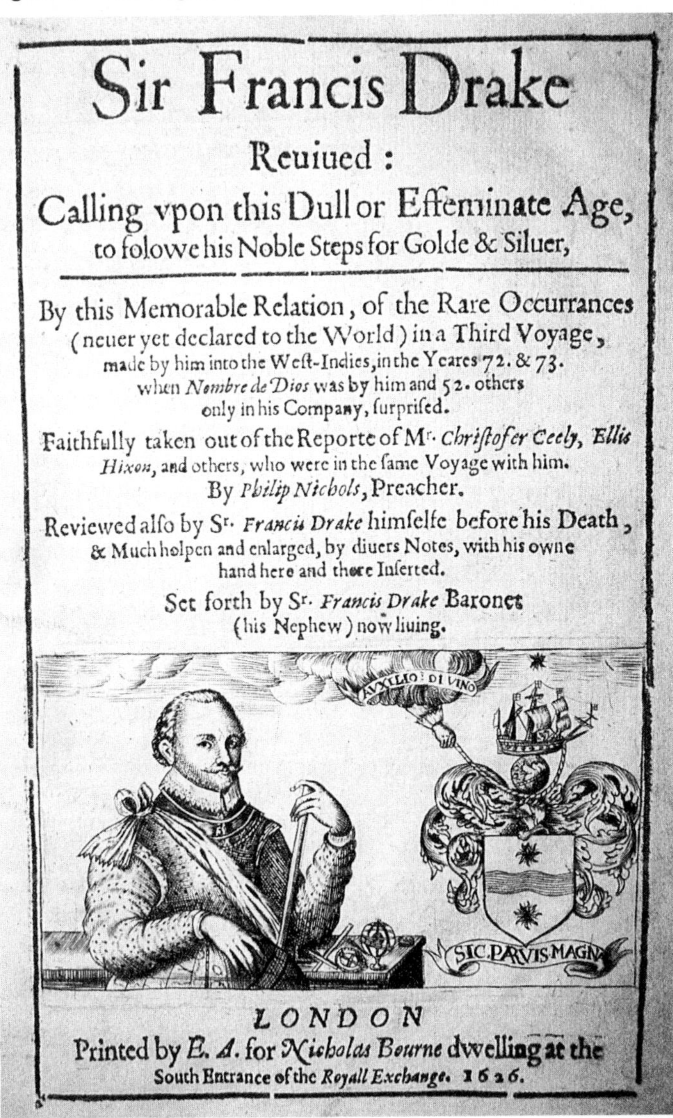

Sir Francis Drake
Reuiued:
Calling vpon this Dull or Effeminate Age,
to folowe his Noble Steps for Golde & Siluer,

By this Memorable Relation, of the Rare Occurrances
(neuer yet declared to the World) in a Third Voyage,
made by him into the West-Indies, in the Yeares 72. & 73.
when *Nombre de Dios* was by him and 52. others
only in his Company, surprised.
Faithfully taken out of the Reporte of Mr. *Christofer Ceely, Ellis Hixon*, and others, who were in the same Voyage with him.
By *Philip Nichols*, Preacher.
Reviewed also by Sr. *Francis Drake* himselfe before his Death,
& Much holpen and enlarged, by diuers Notes, with his owne
hand here and there Inserted.
Set forth by Sr. *Francis Drake* Baronet
(his Nephew) now liuing.

AUXILIO DIVINO
SIC PARVIS MAGNA

LONDON
Printed by *E. A.* for *Nicholas Bourne* dwelling at the
South Entrance of the *Royall Exchange*. 1626.

11 On a map of the world find:

- **a** The Isthmus of Panama.
- **b** Peru, which is where most of the silver mines were.
- **c** Spain, which is where the treasure was taken.

12 Draw a sketch map to show the whole route taken by the treasure.

Note: We know a great deal about Drake's expedition of 1572–1573 from a book called *Sir Francis Drake Revived*. It was written in 1592 by a man called Philip Nichols. He took his information from accounts made by two men who were with Drake. When he had finished his book, Nichols showed it to Drake himself, who added to it and corrected it in a number of places. It then seems to have been forgotten until 1628, when Drake's nephew had it published.

Normally, it would be unwise to trust a book that was printed so long after the events it describes. However, we have letters sent by Spaniards who were in the places Drake raided. These letters agree with *Sir Francis Drake Revived* in all the main facts. It follows that we can believe much, if not everything, that Nichols wrote.

B The Attack on Nombre de Dios

First of all, Drake made for Port Pheasant, which he reached without accident on July 12th 1572. He then had a piece of good luck, for another English ship appeared. Its captain was James Ranse and he had thirty men and a pinnace. Ranse agreed to join forces with Drake. The two commanders decided that Ranse should look after the ships, while Drake led the attack on Nombre de Dios. Accordingly, Drake set off with the four pinnaces, taking 53 of his own men, and 20 of Ranse's. They arrived off the sleeping and unsuspecting town at about two o'clock in the morning of July 19th. What happened next, is described in *Sir Francis Drake Revived*.

Document One

We landed without opposition, although we found one gunner in the very place where we landed, not twenty yards from the houses. There we found six great brass guns, mounted upon their carriages. We at once dismounted them. The gunner fled. The town took alarm as we realised, not only by the noise and cries of the people, but by the bell ringing out and drums running up and down the town. Our Captain left twelve to keep the pinnaces that we might be sure of a safe retreat, if the worse befell. Then he appointed his brother John, with John Oxenham and sixteen other of his men to go about behind the King's treasure-house, and enter near the east end of the market-place. Himself, with the rest, would pass up the main street, into the market-place, with sound of Drum and Trumpet.

Sir Francis Drake Revived

1 What did the English find when they landed?
2 How did they know the alarm had been given?
3 How many men stayed to guard the pinnaces? How many did that leave to attack the town?

Drake and his men now advanced on Nombre de Dios:

Document Two

We had firepikes which not only frightened the enemy, but gave light to our men, who might see every place very well, as if it were day. The inhabitants stood amazed at so strange a sight, and imagining, by reason of our drums and trumpets sounding in different places, that we had been a far greater number than we were.

By now, the soldiers and the inhabitants had put themselves in arms and gathered in the market-place. They presented us with a jolly hot volley of shot, as we came out of the street in which we marched. We stood not to answer them in like terms, but having discharged our first volley of shot and feathered them with our arrows, we came to the push of pike. Partly by reason of our arrows, partly because of this sudden and unexpected closing with them, but mainly because our Captain's brother, with the other company, entered the market-place by the east street they, casting down their weapons fled all out of the town. In following and returning, several of our men were hurt with the weapons which the enemy had let fall as he fled, for they lay thick, and across one another, on the ground.

Sir Francis Drake Revived

1 Why did the Spaniards imagine the English were attacking in large numbers?
2 What Spaniards were there in the market square?
3 With what weapons did Drake's men attack them?
4 What was the main reason the Spaniards fled?
5 Draw a plan of the fighting. Show:
   a The market-square, with roads leading off it, including the main street to the west.
   b The Spaniards.
   c Drake's attack.
   d Drake's brother's attack.
6 Why were several of the English wounded while chasing the enemy?

Figure 1 Drake's men land near Nombre de Dios

According to Nichols, this is what happened after the Spaniards had fled:

Document Three

We then went to the Governor's house where we found the great door open and a candle lighted at the top of the stairs. By means of this light we saw a huge heap of silver in a lower room; being a pile of bars of silver, of (as near as we could guess) seventy feet in length, ten feet in breadth and twelve feet in height, piled against the wall. But our Captain commanded that none of us should touch a bar of silver, but stand upon our weapons, because the town was full of people. Moreover, there was in the King's treasure house, near the water's side, more gold and jewels than all our four pinnaces could carry.

Sir Francis Drake Revived

1 Where did the English find a pile of silver?
2 How big was the pile?
3 Why did Drake forbid his men to touch any of the silver?

Nichols goes on:

Document Four

Soon after this a mighty shower of rain with a terrible storm of thunder and lightning fell, which poured down so hard that before we could take shelter some of our bow strings were wet, as well as some of our powder. At this, several of our men were muttering of the forces of the town, which, when our Captain heard, told them he had brought them to the mouth of the treasure-house of the world, and if they left without it, they should blame nobody but themselves. And therefore, as soon as the storm died down, which took a long half hour, he commanded his brother, with John Oxenham and his company, to break open the King's treasure-house. The rest were to follow him, to keep the enemy out of the square.

But as he stepped forward, he began to faint for want of blood, which, as we saw, he had lost in great quantity from a wound in his leg. He had hidden it from us until his fainting gave him away. The blood filled the very prints that our foot-steps made, to the great dismay of all our company, who thought it impossible that one man should be able to lose so much blood and live.

And therefore, even they that were most willing to have run the greatest dangers for so rich a booty, would not risk their Captain's life. They joined together, and with force mixed with persuasion, they carried him aboard his pinnace. So they abandoned a most rich spoil only to save their Captain's life.

Thus we embarked at break of day, having, besides our Captain, many of our men wounded, though none slain but one Trumpeter.

Sir Francis Drake Revived

1 How did the storm damage the weapons of the English?
2 What did Drake say when he saw his men were frightened?
3 What did Drake order his men to do when the storm was over?
4 Was this order obeyed?
5 How did Drake's men discover he was wounded?
6 Why did the English leave without taking any plunder?
7 How many of the English were killed?

Figure 2 Nombre de Dios, as Drake saw it.

Here now are two Spanish accounts of the fighting in Nombre de Dios:

Document Five

a. At one or two o'clock at night, there entered into the city an armed, attacking party of corsairs, whose presence was not felt until they were ashore and in the streets; and because the people were not prepared, they did much damage and killed certain persons. Being at that time responsible for the defence of the city against corsairs, I was in the market-place with some few persons. And it is certain that if those persons who were in the square for the defence of the city, and in his majesty's service, had not been there, this city would have run very grave risk. Those who were in the market-place were very effective in saving the city from sack and in resisting the corsairs and in driving them back to re-embark.

Statement made at Panama by Antonio Juarez, April 1573

b. A force of about a hundred corsairs entered the city. They began to sound trumpets and to fire artillery (from four pinnaces which they had brought close to the shore) and to fire muskets and arrows through the streets. They killed some men and women, and wounded many more, in all thirty-two persons. Then, in the alarm and turmoil throughout the town, all, or most, of the residents fled into the country.

With six others, I resisted the corsairs, opposing them in the streets, and twice they broke into the market-place. The third time, I and Francisco Ramirez, having called out to the people of the town repeatedly, some of the inhabitants of this city made a stand in the square. There were then some thirty-five or forty men.

I sent a man to learn the enemy's whereabouts, and this man having returned and reported, I came up to the corner of the market-place by the church, there being with me eleven men. There we resisted the corsairs and killed their trumpeter, whose body remained in the market-place, and wounded six or seven others. After which the corsairs withdrew and went to re-embark in their pinnaces.

Statement made at Panama by Garcia de Paz, April 1573

Figure 3 Silver Ingots

According to these Spanish documents:

1. How many English attacked Nombre de Dios?
2. Did the townspeople have any warning of the attack?
3. What weapons did the English use?
4. Did any Spaniards flee from the town?
5. How many Spaniards came to fight in the market-place?
6. Did any of them run away?
7. How many men did Garcia de Paz take to attack the English?
8. Why did the English withdraw?

We will now compare Philip Nichols's *Sir Francis Drake Revived* with the two Spanish accounts. Answer these questions, using both the English and the Spanish sources:

1. Did an English force attack Nombre de Dios?
2. Did it do so at night?
3. Did any Spaniards run away?
4. Was there any fighting on the market-place?
5. Were any Spaniards killed or wounded?
6. Were any of the English killed?
7. Were any of the English wounded?
8. Did the English take any treasure? (The Spaniards are silent on this point. Would they have mentioned loss of treasure, had there been any?)

From your answers to these questions you can see that the English and Spanish accounts agree on a great deal. But now do this exercise. Take a sheet of paper and divide it into three columns. Head the first column *Questions*, the second column *English Accounts* and the third column *Spanish Accounts*. Copy the following questions into the left hand column, and fill in the other two columns for yourself:

1. How many English attacked Nombre de Dios?
2. How much warning did the Spaniards have? (None? a little? plenty?)
3. What weapons did the English use?
4. Who won the fight on the market-place?
5. How were the English wounded?
6. Why did the English withdraw?

The biggest problem with Philip Nicols's account is his mention of the treasure. We can be sure Drake thought there was treasure in Nombre de Dios, or he would never have attacked the town. From other records we can also be sure that the treasure had left for Spain several weeks before the English arrived. It is hard to understand, then, why Nichols says that Drake's men found a huge heap of silver. There are a number of possibilities.

Perhaps there was indeed some silver, though there cannot have been nearly as much as Nichols suggests. Perhaps there was something that looked like silver, though it is difficult to imagine what it might be. Perhaps Nichols, or the men who told him the story of the raid were lying. Think about these suggestions and any other ideas which you might have.

C Drake and the Cimarrones

After the fiasco at Nombre de Dios, Ranse went his own way. As for Drake, he and his men sailed up and down the coast of the Isthmus of Panama, looking for plunder. All they managed to do was take a few small ships carrying supplies, such as food and wine. Several men were killed in these actions, including Drake's brother, John. Even more died from disease. Drake had left England with 73 men and boys, but by early in 1573, only 30 were still alive. Then the English met a people known as the Cimarrones.

The Cimarrones were black slaves who had escaped from the Spaniards. There may have been as many as 3000 of them. They built themselves villages in the jungle where they lived, mainly by hunting. Philip Nichols describes one of these villages, which he calls a town:

Document One

Around the Town is a ditch eight feet wide and a thick mud wall of ten feet high, enough to stop a sudden surprise. It has one long and broad street lying east and west, and two other cross streets of lesser breadth and length. There were in it some fifty-five houses which were kept so clean and sweet that not only the houses, but the very streets were very pleasant to behold.

The Town is well stored with many sorts of beasts and fowls, with plenty of maize and with different kinds of fruits.

Their hunting arrows are of three sorts. The first serveth to kill any great beast near at hand, as ox, stag or wild boar. This hath a head of iron of a pound and a half weight, shaped like a javelin, as sharp as any knife, making so large and deep a wound as can hardly be believed by him that hath not seen it. The second serveth for smaller beasts and hath a head of three quarters of a pound. The third serveth for all manner of birds. It hath a head of an ounce weight.

Their constant need for these arrows means they think far more highly of iron than they do of gold.

Sir Francis Drake Revived

1 How is the village defended?
2 How many streets are there?
3 How many houses are there? How do the Cimarrones keep them?

Drake was lucky to find the Cimarrones, for they knew the country well. They also knew the habits of the Spaniards. They told Drake that the best way to capture some Spanish treasure would be to ambush one of the mule trains that carried it from Panama to Nombre de Dios. The mule trains began their journeys when the treasure fleet arrived at Nombre de Dios. This was usually some time in January. The Cimarrones offered to keep watch for the English, and soon they reported that the treasure fleet had arrived. Drake now hoped to ambush a mule train, so an expedition set out to cross the Isthmus of Panama. Nichols wrote:

Document Two

We were in all forty-eight, of which eighteen only were English. The rest were Cimarrones, which besides their arms, took every one of them a great quantity of food and equipment. They carried all the things we needed in so long a march, so that we were not troubled with anything but our weapons. Yea, many times when some of our company fainted with sickness or weariness, two Cimarrones would carry him with ease.

Sir Francis Drake Revived

1 How many men were there in the expedition? How many were English? How many were Cimarrones?
2 What did the Cimarrones carry? What did the English carry?
3 What happened if one of the Englishmen was unable to walk?

This is how the expedition managed for food:

Document Three

Because the Cimarrones could not carry enough

food, they kept us supplied with their arrows. When they found any wild pigs, six of them would give their loads to the rest of their fellows, and pursue, kill and bring away after us as much as they could carry. One day as we travelled, the Cimarrones found an otter and prepared it for cooking. Our Captain marvelling at it, the chief Cimarron asked him, 'Are you a man of war and hungry, and yet doubt that this be meat that hath blood?' At this our Captain rebuked himself secretly, that he had scorned to eat such food.
Sir Francis Drake Revived

1 How did the Cimarrones provide food?
2 What meat was Drake unwilling to eat, at first?

This is how the expedition marched:

Figure 1 English and Cimarrones in the Jungle

Document Four
This was the order of our march: Four of those Cimarrones that best knew the ways went about a mile before us, breaking boughs as they went, to be a direction to those that followed, but with great silence. Then twelve of them were our vanguard and twelve our rearguard, we with their two captains in the middle.
Sir Francis Drake Revived

Note: 'vanguard' – troops that go ahead of the main body, to prevent it from being surprised

1 Why did four Cimarrones go ahead of the expedition?
2 Could any of the English have done this work?
3 Draw a diagram to show the order of march. (You could use black dots for the Cimarrones, and small white circles for the English.)
4 Which group ran the greater danger, do you suppose, the English or the Cimarrones?

After eleven days the expedition was close to Panama. Here is what happened:

Document Five
We sent a Cimarron, one that had served a master in Panama, to go into the town to learn the night when the carriers took the treasure from Panama to Nombre de Dios. Soon he returned to tell us, that which very happily he understood from friends of his: that the Treasurer of Lima, intending to go to Spain, was ready that night to take his journey towards Nombre de Dios, having fourteen mules of which eight were laden with gold and one with jewels. And further, that there were two other mule trains, laden with food, to come forth that night after the other.
Sir Francis Drake Revived

1 Why was a Cimarron sent into Panama?
2 Why was this particular man chosen?
3 What news did he bring from Panama?
4 Could any of the English have done the same as this Cimarron?

D Ambushing the Mule Trains

As you have already seen, Drake's men and the Cimarrones made a difficult and dangerous journey across the Isthmus of Panama. They arrived safely and made the happy discovery that three mule trains were about to leave Panama, one of them carrying a load of gold and jewels. Since the expedition had travelled in secret, the Spaniards suspected nothing, and it should not have been too difficult to capture this mule train. Drake laid an ambush:

> *Document One*
>
> Being at the chosen place our Captain with half of his men lay on one side of the track, about fifty paces off in the long grass. John Oxenham, with the other half, lay on the other side of the track at the same distance. Now though there was as great charge given as might be that none of our men should show or stir themselves, yet one of our men called Robert Pike, having drunk too much aqua vitae, forgot himself. Persuading a Cimarron to come with him, he went close to the road, meaning to be the first to seize the mules. And when a horseman from Venta Cruz passed by, foolishly he rose up to see what he was. The Cimarron, who had more sense, pulled him down and lay upon him. Yet the horseman had taken notice, seeing one all in white, for we had put our shirts over our other clothes, so that we might be sure to know our own men in the pell mell of the night. Having seen this the horseman, putting spurs to his horse, rode at a fast gallop to give warning.
>
> *Sir Francis Drake Revived*

Note: 'aqua vitae' – a strong spirit, like whisky or brandy

1 How did Drake divide his force?
2 Where did his men lie?
3 What strict instructions did Drake give his men?
4 What had Robert Pike been doing?
5 Where did he go? Why?
6 What did he do when he heard a horseman?
7 Why was it easy for the horseman to see Pike?

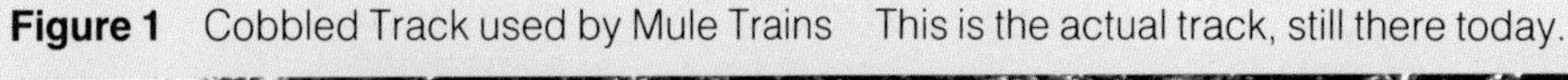

Figure 1 Cobbled Track used by Mule Trains This is the actual track, still there today.

8 What did the horseman do when he saw him?

The horseman had seen only one man, for a second or two, so the Spaniards could not be sure there was an ambush. What they did was to halt the mule train which was carrying the gold and jewels, and send forward one of the others. Drake's party ambushed it, only to find they had captured, not treasure, but food.

The English now had to return to their ships. They reached them exhausted and downhearted. Drake, though, was still determined to find some treasure, so he began, once again, to sail up and down the coast. Then he had yet another stroke of good fortune. He met a French captain, Guillaume le Testu, who had a large ship and seventy men. Drake and le Testu agreed to work together.

This time it was decided to ambush a mule train as it neared the end of its journey. A force of fifteen Englishmen, twenty Frenchmen and some Cimarrones made their way inland. Philip Nichols describes the ambush:

Document Two

There came three mule trains, one of fifty mules, the other two of seventy each, every one of which carried 300 pounds weight of silver, which in all amounted to nearly 30 tons. We went down to the road and took hold of the first and last mules, and all the rest stopped and lay down, as their manner is. These three trains were guarded with forty-five soldiers, fifteen to each train, which caused some exchange of bullets and arrows for a time. In this conflict the French captain was badly wounded in the belly, and one Cimarron slain. But in the end those soldiers thought it best to leave their mules with us, and go for help. In the mean time we eased some of the mules of their burdens. Being weary, we were contented with as few bars and pieces of gold, as we could well carry. We buried about fifteen tons of silver, partly in the burrows which the great land-crabs had made in the earth, and partly under old trees which had fallen, and partly in the sand and gravel of a river. Thus when we had spent some two hours about this business we began our march back through the woods. The French captain, not able to travel further because of his wound, stayed in the hope that some rest would recover him better strength.

But after we had marched some two leagues, the French complained that they missed one of their private soldiers. It was found he had drunk much wine, and overloading himself with plunder, and hasting to go before us, had lost himself in the woods. And, as we afterward discovered, he was taken by the Spaniards that evening and, upon torture, told them where we had hidden our treasure.

Sir Francis Drake Revived

1 How many mules were there?

2 How much silver was each one carrying?

3 How was the mule train stopped?

4 What happened to Captain le Testu?

5 The ambush party did not take away much treasure. Why?

6 What did they do with the treasure they left behind?

7 How did one of the Frenchmen get lost?

8 What did he tell the Spaniards?

Most of the English and French reached their ships safely. Two weeks later, Drake sent John Oxenham with some men to recover the hidden treasure and, if possible, rescue Captain le Testu. They found that the Spaniards had dug up all the silver, except thirteen bars which Oxenham brought back to the ship. As for le Testu, he had been killed.

Drake divided the booty with the French, but that still left him with a small fortune, so he sailed for home. He reached Plymouth on a Sunday. The parson was in the middle of his sermon, but the congregation rose in a body and left. Philip Nichols wrote: 'The news of our captain's return overcame their minds with desire and delight to see him. All hastened to see the proof of God's love towards our Gracious Queen and Country, by the fruit of our captain's labour and success.'

5 John Oxenham's Expedition to the Isthmus of Panama, 1576–1577

A Oxenham arrives in the Isthmus of Panama

When he went to the isthmus of Panama in 1572, Drake had with him a man called John Oxenham. In 1576, Oxenham decided to organise an expedition of his own. Eventually, he was captured by the Spaniards, who asked him why he had come. This was his answer:

Document One
Captain Drake, who sailed along these coasts, told me that in Vallano there were Cimarrones, rich in gold and silver. He said I could barter with them whatever I might bring. And I came, meaning to barter with the negroes. I brought cloth, hatchets, machetes and other things I intended to barter for gold and silver.
Deposition of John Oxenham at Ronconcholon, October 20th, 1577

Note: 'machete' – large, heavy knife

1 Oxenham says Drake told him about the Cimarrones. In fact, Oxenham had been with Drake in 1572–1573. Why did he not admit this, do you suppose?
2 Did Oxenham really believe the Cimarrones had any treasure, do you think?
3 How, in fact, did Oxenham mean to get treasure, do you think?

When he first arrived in the West Indies, Oxenham captured two small sailing ships, called frigates. He then hid his own ship and put together two pinnaces he had brought with him. The party set off in these pinnaces and the frigates, hoping to meet some Cimarrones. After a while they found two, who promised to take them to their village of Ronconcholon, which was in a remote area called Vallano.

Oxenham hid his pinnaces and anchored the frigates in a natural harbour. He left some men to guard them, and build a fort, while he and the rest went to Ronconcholon.

Unfortunately for Oxenham, some of the Spaniards he had captured in the frigates managed to escape. They told Dr. Loarte, the governor of the area about Oxenham. Loarte describes what happened next:

Document Two
I sent a brigantine along the north coast, with a captain and soldiers. He found two frigates anchored in the harbour called Pinas. He fired on them with his artillery, saw those on board escape to land, grappled with the frigates and took them.
On shore, they had begun to build a fort. This he burnt, and came back with the frigates.
On board the frigates and in the fort there was a quantity of cloth and linens and some silks, and many storm-coats of the sort the French and English wear, iron-work for ships, ropes, and the anchors of their own ships. There were also found seven good guns and some ammunition.
Dr. Loarte to the Crown, 26th April, 1577

Note: 'brigantine' – small sailing vessel

1 Whom did Loarte send to look for Oxenham?
2 What did Oxenham's men do when the Spaniards arrived?
3 What did the Spaniards do to the fort?
4 What did they do with the frigates?
5 What did they find in the frigates and the fort?

Meanwhile, Oxenham was at Ronconcholon with the Cimarrones. Later, he told his Spanish captors:

Figure 1 Spanish Frigate

> *Document Three*
> While I was at Ronconcholon, I heard that the Spaniards had taken all the goods I had for barter and my food, and nine guns, and the gunpowder and ammunition I had brought. The Spaniards also took the swords and weapons that we had in the frigates, so we were disarmed and discouraged. Seeing I had no food or arms or ammunition, with which to return to my own country, nor goods to trade with the negroes, as I had promised them, I remained quiet in the village and sent for my men.
> *Deposition of John Oxenham*, October 20th, 1577

1 According to Oxenham, what did he lose to the Spaniards?

2 Does Oxenham's list agree, roughly, with Loarte's?

3 According to Oxenham, what was he now unable to do?

4 What action did he take?

Although the Spaniards had recaptured their frigates, Oxenham still had the ship in which he had sailed from England. But he was now to lose this as well, and in rather a strange way. He said:

> *Document Four*
> The negroes told me that if I wanted them to provide me and my men with food, I must burn my ship, and give them its iron and nails. They also said that if I did this, they would take me to the Pacific, and help me to take much gold and silver, provided I would kill all the Spaniards I captured and give them any negroes I might get. Since I had no way of finding food, I had to agree to all these conditions.
> *Deposition of John Oxenham*, October 20th, 1577

Note: Iron was very valuable to the Cimarrones, who used it to make arrows.

1 What did the Cimarrones want from Oxenham's ship?

2 What was the only way to get it?

3 Where did the Cimarrones promise to take Oxenham? What did they say they would help him do there?

4 What did Oxenham promise to do with

- **a** any Spaniards he might capture and
- **b** any negroes he might find?

B The Raid on the Pearl Islands

Oxenham burnt his ship, and gave the nails and iron in it to the Cimarrones, as he had promised. The Cimarrones then helped the English to build a pinnace, which they floated down a river, and out to sea. It was a historic moment, for Oxenham and his followers were the first Englishmen to sail on the Pacific Ocean. Probably, though, they were far more interested in where they were going. This was to the Pearl Islands, a group of islands just off the coast, where the Spaniards sent negro slaves to dive for pearls.

As no Europeans but themselves had ever sailed on the Pacific, the Spaniards on the Pearl Islands were amazed when the English landed. Later, one of them said:

Document One

A negress, my slave, opened the door at the dogs' barking, and ran back into the house crying, 'My lady, the French!' They beat at the door and I came down, and a crowd of them entered the house. I recognised them as English. They seated me in a chair and the negro Juan Vaquero, who was leader of the Cimarrones, threw an iron collar about my neck, and took his machete to strike me. I appealed to the English not to let a negro mistreat me, and they prevented it, and held me until their captain arrived.

Deposition of Juan de Manzaneda, Panama, April 17th, 1577

Figure 1 Pearl in Oyster Shell

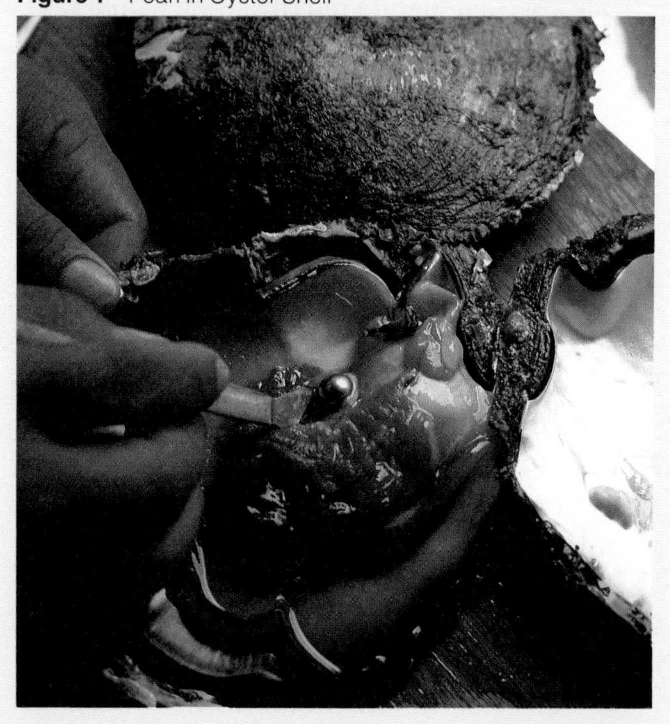

1 For whom did the negress mistake Oxenham's men?

2 What was Juan Vaquero going to do? Who stopped him?

All the English in Oxenham's party were Protestants. They hated the Roman Catholic religion to which the Spaniards belonged. As a result, they not only robbed the Spaniards, but insulted their religion. One of the Spaniards said:

Document Two

I was with my wife and children on one of the Pearl Islands when a launch arrived and in it about fifty Englishmen. They had with them nine Cimarrones and an Indian. They ordered me to give them gold, silver and pearls.

After they had taken from me everything I had, they found certain books, among them a pontifical. They asked me why I had those books, which were all lies, adding that the pope was a ____ and that I should not believe in him. Having found a child's lesson book, one of the English named Chalona, who is the interpreter among them, stopped to read it. He was reading the ten commandments, when he came to the commandment, 'Thou shalt not steal.' He laughed loudly at it, and said that all goods were common property; and all of them laughed and jeered at the commandments. Next, the English captain found a crucifix. He looked at me angrily and said, 'Why have you got this?' He threw it at me, but it missed me and struck a stand which broke the crucifix to pieces.

So also they found a holy picture. The captain took a dagger and struck the picture two blows in the face, and slashed it with the blade, and ripped it from the board on which it was, and broke off a piece and threw it upon

the floor and trampled upon it.
Deposition of Diego de Sotomayor, Panama, April 17th, 1577

1 What did the English say about the pope?
2 What made Chalona laugh? Why was that, do you suppose?
3 What did Oxenham do to the crucifix and the holy picture?

These are some more complaints that Sotomayor made about the English:

Document Three
They then went to Juan Manzaneda's house, where I saw they had smashed the altar he had there for the celebration of mass, and thrown it down at the kitchen door. The English cook took the alb used in the ceremony of the mass, and put it on and danced about in it, ridiculing everything. Afterwards, he cut the alb short and kept it on for a shirt. The English used the church for a kitchen and burnt the images which were in it. And because a little girl brought out a picture of Mary Magdalene and put out the flames that were burning it, they threatened her, and told her to drop it, and called her a troublesome brat.
Deposition of Diego de Sotomayor, Panama, April 17th, 1577

Note: 'alb' – long, white garment worn by a priest

1 What did the English do to the altar?
2 What did the cook do to the alb?
3 How did the English use the church?
4 What was the little girl trying to do? What did the English say to her?

Here is something else that happened:

Document Four
During this time Juan Constantino, priest and commissary of the holy office of the Inquisition, and a Franciscan friar with him, arrived at the island. They removed Constantino's hat and because his head was not shaven, they let him alone. But all the Englishmen took the friar and hit him, and put a chamber-pot upon his head, and struck him many fisticuffs upon the head. The friar was humble, exclaiming, 'So be it, for the love of God.' They seated him in a chair, saying to him, 'You are God, to confess and forgive sins' and, mocking him, they knelt before him and talked to him in Latin.

The next day they showed the friar a wooden cross and asked him what it was. When the friar said it was the image of the cross upon which Jesus Christ, Our Lord, was crucified, the English replied, 'Well, that's where we will hang you and burn you before we go.' To which the friar answered that he did not deserve so much honour; and at this they left him alone.
Deposition of Diego de Sotomayor, Panama, April 17th, 1577

Figure 2 Friar

1 Why did the English leave Juan Constantino alone?
2 Name some of the ways in which they ill-treated and insulted the friar.
3 What did the English threaten to do to the friar? Did they carry out this threat?

C The Capture of a Treasure Ship

Having looted the Pearl Islands, Oxenham decided to capture one of the ships bringing treasure from Peru to Panama. As we have seen, the Spaniards did not expect to meet enemies in the Pacific. They were easily surprised and Oxenham took a ship without difficulty. The Town Council of Panama wrote to the King of Spain:

Document One

Today a bark reached this city from Guayaquil. The English had looted it. It had on board more than 70,000 pesos in gold belonging to your majesty and private persons, and a great quantity of biscuit, bacon and cheese and shoes and gunpowder: all of which the English were lacking and in great need. These people who were robbed brought the news that the corsairs had departed the night before. Immediately the fleet which the governor, Dr. Loarte, had raised, went after them. Pedro de Ortega is in command of it. He went to the gulf, searching all the rivers which the English entered. The governor sent another forty men overland by way of the mountain range, to cut off their retreat. Everything humanly possible has been done.

City of Panama to the Crown, April 15th, 1577

1 What had the English taken from the Spanish ship?
2 How recently had the English parted from the Spaniards they had robbed?
3 In your opinion, was Oxenham wise to release his captives so soon?
4 What action did Dr. Loarte take?

In 1593 an Englishman, Sir Richard Hawkins, was captured by the Spaniards and sent to prison in Peru. While he was there he heard this story about Oxenham:

Document Two

With the help of the Cimarrones he built a small pinnace. He fitted it in warlike manner, and put himself into the South Sea. His good luck was to meet a ship carrying a great quantity of gold. And among other things there were two pieces of great worth. One was a table of gold, with emeralds, sent for a present to the king; the other was a Lady of singular beauty, married and a mother of children. The

Figure 1 Cimarrones ill-treating Spanish Captives. This was the fate from which Oxenham and his men wanted to save the Spaniards they had captured.

latter was his downfall.

For he had agreed with the Cimarrones that their part of the booty should be the prisoners, so that they could take their revenge upon them. Such was their hatred, that they used to roast and eat the hearts of all those Spaniards, whom at any time they could lay hand upon. John Oxenham (I say) was taken with the love of this Lady and to win her good will, what through her tears and persuasions, breaking promise with the Cimarrones, agreed to her request. This was to give the prisoners liberty with their ships, since they were no use to him. None the less, Oxenham kept the Lady.

The rest of the Spaniards made all the haste they could to Panama. There, the governor acted so quickly that within a few hours troops were sent to seek the English, who little thought to be so quickly overtaken.

The Observations of Sir Richard Hawkins, 1622

1. What did Oxenham find on the ship he captured, as well as treasure?
2. What had he promised to give the Cimarrones?
3. What foolish action did Oxenham take? Why?
4. What were the Spaniards in Panama able to do as a result?

Unfortunately, we do not know how much of Richard Hawkins's story we can believe. He was only repeating gossip he heard sixteen years after Oxenham captured the treasure ship, and what is more, his account was not printed until 1622. But see if Documents One and Two give the same answers to these questions:

1. Did Oxenham capture a treasure ship?
2. Did he release the crew, with their ship, very soon afterwards?
3. Did the Spaniards in Panama go after the English very promptly?

Your answers should show that the Spanish document, written just after the events took place, agrees in important ways with Hawkins's account.

D Ortega's Campaign

As you have seen, the Spanish general who went after Oxenham was Pedro de Ortega. He was close behind the English, but he still had to find their trail. He was nearly sure they had gone inland by a certain river, but it had three mouths and he did not know which one to enter. Richard Hawkins wrote:

Document One

The pursuers, approaching the river, were doubtful which of its three mouths they should take. Then one of the soldiers saw some hens' feathers and some boughs of trees (which they had cut off to make their way) swimming down one of the outlets. This was light enough to guide them in their course. They entered the river and followed the track, as far as their frigates had enough water. And then, with part of their soldiers in their boats, and the rest on the banks on either side, they marched day and night in pursuit of their enemies. They came upon them at the head of the river, making good cheer in their tents, and arguing about the sharing of their gold. Thus they were surprised and not one escaped.

The Observations of Sir Richard Hawkins, 1622

According to Hawkins:

1. How did the Spaniards know which river mouth to enter?
2. Where did they find Oxenham's party? What happened to it?

The Town Council of Panama wrote to the King of Spain:

Document Two

Guided by God, they went up a stream which they were eight days in ascending. When his vessels could go no higher, the general landed with 60 of his soldiers and pressed on into the mountains. He found the trail of the English, who had left pork and biscuits where they had stopped to eat. After four days journey, they heard two harquebus shots. The general ordered a soldier to go into the bush to discover what this meant. On the river bank he saw some thirty English and more that eighty negroes who were cooking pork and amusing themselves together. They had an awning stretched, where they were unloading the biscuit and everything else they had in the launch. The soldier returned to report to the general.

Having encouraged his soldiers like a most Christian captain, the general ordered them to offer a prayer to God, our Lord. Then, in complete silence, they came up through the trees and gave the enemy the first volley. It killed more than twenty-five of the English, and many of the negroes, who fled with some of the English.

The City of Panama to the Crown, April 26th, 1577

1 According to the Town Council of Panama, who guided Ortega's men into the right stream?
2 How did the Spaniards follow the trail of the English, inland?
3 How did they know when they were close to the English?
4 What did the Spanish scout discover?
5 What happened when the Spaniards attacked?
6 What should Oxenham have done, do you think, to prevent his party being surprised in this way?
7 In what way does the Spanish account disagree with Hawkins's? (Look at the last sentences in *Documents One* and *Two*.)

The letter from the Town Council of Panama goes on:

Document Three

Ortega continued his march in search of the enemy and arrived at the village of the negroes. There the English captain, with the Cimarrones and what men he had left, awaited attack in his fort.

Calling on our patron, the Apostle St. James, the general stormed the fort and in a long hour's fight killed many of the enemy and wounded most of the rest. Ours suffered little damage, for the enemy had few harquebuses, being mostly armed with bows and arrows. The

Figure 1 Spanish Soldiers

Figure 2 Chagres River It was up this river that Oxenham sailed.

Figure 3 British Army Tent, Belize, 1985 Oxenham and his men slept in shelters which the Cimarrones made from branches and leaves. Today, British soldiers use tents like this, when they are in the jungle. Why are they raised off the ground, do you suppose?

enemy abandoned the village and fled into the bush, where they will have died, being wounded. Having seen what damage they have received on account of the English, the negroes will have killed any survivors. The general captured three boys and an Englishman who was shot through the leg.
The City of Panama to the Crown, April 26th 1577

1 Where had the English and Cimarrones taken refuge?
2 What did Ortega succeed in doing?
3 Why were few of the Spaniards hurt?
4 According to this letter, why are none of the English still alive?
5 What prisoners did the Spaniards take?

Here is what happened after the battle:

Document Four
Having won the victory, the general at once looked for the booty the enemy had carried off. He exerted pressure on one of the boys he had captured who said he would lead him to the place where they had buried it.

They dug and found twenty-seven bags of gold and thirty-three of silver, and thirteen bars, which was all that the English took from the bark that came from Guayaquil. They found also more gold and silver which they had got from other robberies they had committed on the Atlantic. All this was brought before the general who rendered greater service in defending it from his friends and soldiers than in retaking it from his enemies!

General Pedro de Ortega deserves from your majesty honour and reward for defeating John Oxenham. For had Oxenham succeeded, it would have meant the total ruin of this realm. We are certain that every man of John Oxenham's company would have equipped a vessel in his own country to return here.
The City of Panama to the Crown. April 26th, 1577

1 Who told Ortega where the treasure was buried? Why? ('Exerted pressure' is probably a polite phrase for something very unpleasant. What was that, do you think?)
2 What did Ortega have to prevent his men from doing?
3 According to the Town Council of Panama, what would have happened if Oxenham had succeeded, that is, returned home with the treasure?

E The Fate of the English and the Cimarrones

Even after Ortega's victory, there were still about thirty English at large. Another Spanish commander, Diego de Frias, went to find them. By now the English were in difficulty, for the Cimarrones had turned against them. Later, Oxenham told the Spaniards.

Document One
They treated us very badly and would give us nothing, because we had not killed the Spaniards we captured. The negroes kept scolding us for this, saying that we were to blame for their ruin, in that we did not kill the Spaniards. If we had done so, they would not have followed them and defeated them. For which reason, the negroes gave us no food and no clothing, and we were all naked and hungry.
Deposition of John Oxenham, October 1577

1 Why did the Cimarrones refuse to help the English?

Frias's men found numbers of the English, including Oxenham. He describes his own capture:

Document Two
I was hiding with four men, when I learnt that a party was advancing through the bush. One day I saw some men, and knew they had seen me. I fled, trying to hide behind a tree, but could not reach it. I saw a soldier and a negro. The soldier was armed with a sword and shield and the negro with a bow and arrows. I gripped a lance and advanced on them, and they fell back.

And while I was trying to hide, I saw another soldier with a harquebus aimed at me, and ready to fire. I threw up my hands and cried, 'For the love of God, don't kill me!' He ordered me to drop my lance, which I did. Instantly, many soldiers came and seized me. They gave me many blows, and knife wounds on the head.
Deposition of John Oxenham, July 1578

Later, a Spanish official wrote to the King:

Document Three
About twenty days ago, General de Frias took five other English. Among them is Chalona, who enabled the rest to cross to the Pacific, because he is a clever man. He has promised to lead the general to where he will find the English who are missing, and try to lay hands on Juan Vaquero, captain of the negroes.
Pedro de Busto to the Crown, March 1578

Note: Chalona's real name was Butler. He was Oxenham's second-in-command.

1 What did Butler promise the Spaniards?
2 Why did he do this, do you think?

After some weeks in the bush, Frias's men returned to Panama. They brought with them eighteen English prisoners and forty negroes. Some of the English were still free, led by a man the Spaniards called Canoa. According to one report, they reached the coast and stole a ship. Also, they promised the Cimarrones living in Vallano that they would come back with a strong army.

As for the eighteen who were captured, thirteen were executed in Panama. Oxenham, Butler and three others were kept for questioning. They were executed three years later. Richard Hawkins said this was God's punishment on them since they had broken their promise to the Cimarrones, and Oxenham had fallen in love with another man's wife.

Frias had orders to punish the Cimarrones. Here is part of his report:

Document Four
I fell upon Anton Mandinga's village and burned it and captured his women and children. All their possessions and food supplies were destroyed. Their camps and their crops were destroyed. I have done all I could to serve your Majesty in this campaign, to the point where not a negro remains in the bush, except he be in hiding. Well punished are these blacks, and sorry they ever let the English pass!
Diego de Frias to the Crown, February 1578

Figure 1 The Capture of Oxenham

1 What did the Spaniards do to the village?
2 Whom did they capture?
3 How else did they harm the Cimarrones?

The following year, an official in Panama wrote to the King:

Document Five
The Cimarrones of Puerto Bello, who asked for peace after those of Vallano had done so, have shown themselves more in earnest. A site is already chosen for their village a league and a half from Nombre de Dios. They have been given letters of freedom and clothing. Nothing remains except to fetch their maize and belongings by sea, and bring in their women. This will be done very shortly. Having promised to make peace, the blacks of Vallano have revolted. Seeing they had not kept their agreements, troops were sent against them.
De Villanueva to the Crown, October 1579

1 Which Cimarrones have made peace with the Spaniards?
2 Where are they going to live?
3 What have they been given?
4 What other help will they have?
5 What promise have the Cimarrones of Vallano broken?
6 What action have the Spaniards taken against them?

Probably, the Cimarrones of Vallano were hoping Canoa would return. He had said he would arrive in a ship flying a black flag. They watched for it in vain. When they had waited long enough, they too made peace.

6 The Defeat of the Spanish Armada

A Introduction

1 John Hawkins

If you read Chapter 2, you learnt something about John Hawkins. In 1573, he gave up going to sea for a time. Instead, he worked for the Queen as Treasurer of the Navy. It is now 1588 and King Philip II of Spain has prepared a great fleet, or Armada, to invade England. We will ask Hawkins about it.

'Why do the Spaniards want to invade England?'

'Most of the English are Protestants. The Spaniards want to make us Catholics. When our Queen's sister, Mary, was on the throne, she wanted to do the same. Her way of turning the country Catholic was to burn a good many Protestants alive at Smithfield. We were only too thankful when Mary died and Elizabeth became Queen. If the Spaniards conquer England, they will put a Catholic monarch on the throne. Then the fires of Smithfield will burn again.'

Figure 1 Ships of Henry VIII Note the tall castles on them.

'What are you doing to defend your country?'

'For many years, those of us who look after the navy have been building warships. The Queen now has a fleet of 43 ships. Eighteen of these are powerful galleons. Moreover, they are made to a new design.'

'Please tell us about it.'

'I should start by explaining that in the days before gunpowder, ships could do little damage to each other. To attack a ship, you first of all grappled with her. That meant flinging hooks on the ends of ropes into her. You then pulled her against your own ship, and tied the two together. Your men then boarded the enemy ship, hoping to overpower her crew. You see, you did not sink an enemy ship. You captured her by grappling and boarding.'

'But ships have had cannon for a long time.'

'Yes, and very big some of them are. We have guns that will fire shot weighing fifty or sixty pounds. That will do dreadful damage. But men have been slow to give up grappling and boarding. They have even built higher and higher castles on their ships. That makes them better for the old way of fighting. This was done in the English navy during the reign of the Queen's father, Henry VIII. Some of Henry's ships were so tall that they were top heavy. They would capsize in a flat calm. We all know what happened to the *Mary Rose*! The Spaniards know better than to build ships like the *Mary Rose*. But they still make their castles as tall as they dare.'

'It seems that you dislike tall castles.'

'A ship with tall castles does not sail well.

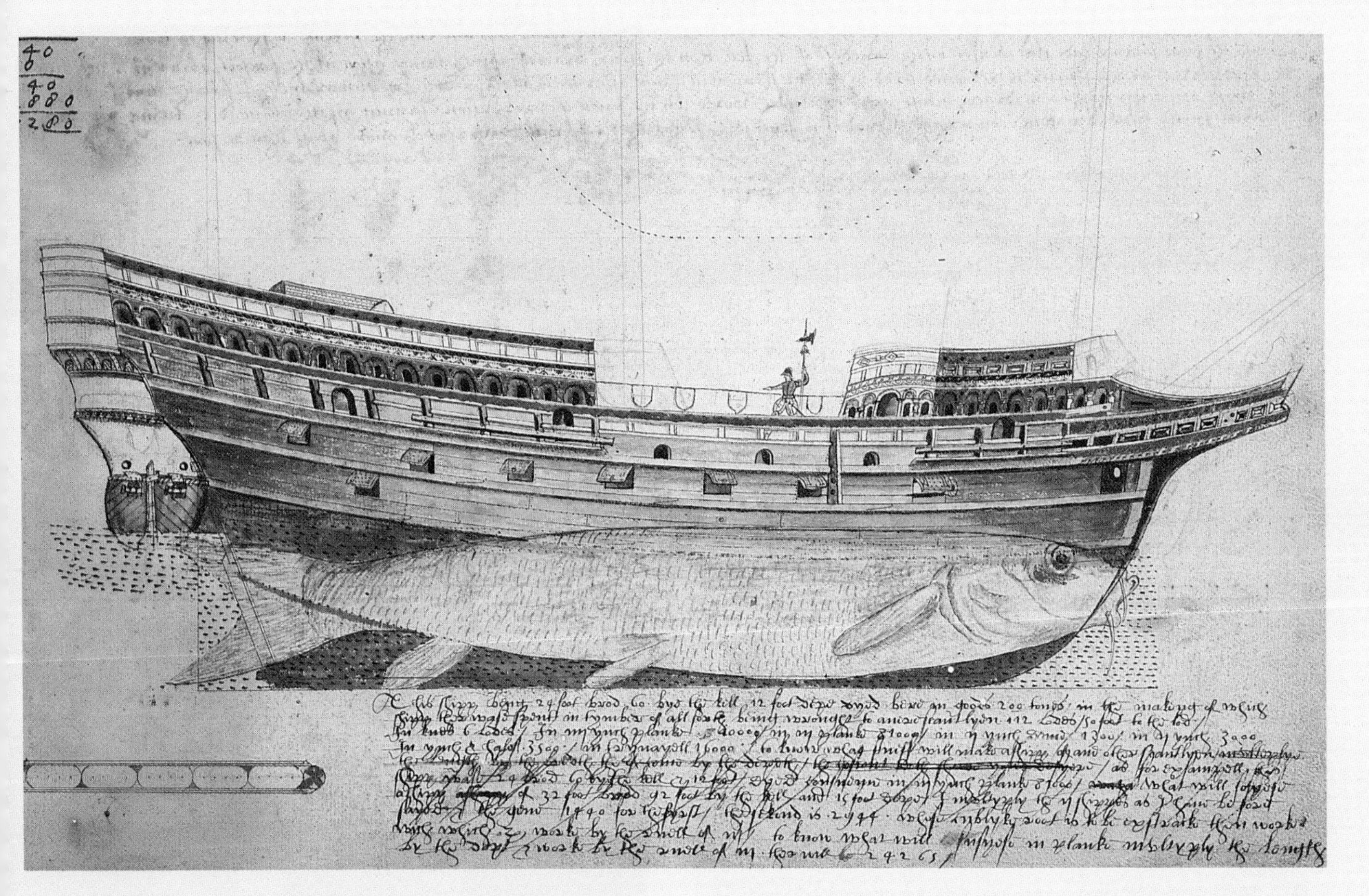

Figure 2 Design for an Elizabethan Warship Compare the castles with those on Henry VIII's ships. What shape is the hull, below the water line?

She pitches and rolls. Even more important, she is slow and difficult to manoeuvre.'

'How have you designed your ships, then?'

'I have cut down the height of the castles. I have made the hulls narrower in relation to their width. Under the water, I have given them the shape of a fish. My ships are easy to manoeuvre, and they are fast. They will outsail the Spanish ships quite easily.'

Figure 3 Model of an Elizabethan Warship

'How will you fight with your new ships?'

'We will keep out of the range of the Spaniards' heavy guns, and we will bombard their ships from a safe distance.'

'You have given up the whole idea of grappling and boarding, then?'

'Yes, we will try to disable or even sink our enemies, instead.'

'When do you think the Spaniards will come?'

'They had hoped the Armada would sail last year. But Sir Francis Drake took a fleet to Cadiz and burnt a great many ships there. This delayed the Spaniards for months. Drake called his raid "singeing the King of Spain's beard." Now, we are expecting to hear any day that the Spaniards have sailed. I wish they would hurry. Keeping the fleet ready for battle is expensive. Soon the government will run out of money, and our men will have neither pay nor food.'

'Who do you think is going to win?'

'We shall.'

'You have a lot of faith in your ships!'

'Yes. But I have even more faith in God. He is on the side of the true Protestant religion.'

1. According to Hawkins, why do the Spaniards want to invade England?
2. How many warships have been built to defend England?
3. What are 'grappling' and 'boarding'?
4. Why have ships been built with high castles?
5. What is wrong with such ships?
6. Name three ways in which Hawkins has improved the design of ships.
7. In what ways are they better than Spanish ships?
8. How will the English fight with their new ships?
9. What will they try to do, instead of grappling and boarding?
10. What did Drake do at Cadiz? How did he describe his raid?
11. Why does Hawkins want the Spaniards to attack soon?
12. Why does Hawkins think the English will win?

Figure 4 Philip II of Spain

2 Philip II of Spain

We will now discuss the war with the King of Spain.

'Your Majesty, why do you wish to invade England?'

'To restore her to the Roman Catholic faith. Under Elizabeth, England is a Protestant country. Catholics are cruelly persecuted there.'

'But Elizabeth became Queen thirty years ago. Why have you waited so long?'

'I did not want a war with England. Besides, it seemed for a time that if we waited, all would be well.'

'Why was that?'

'Elizabeth is not married and has no children. The heir to the throne was her cousin, Mary, Queen of Scots. She was a Catholic. As soon as Elizabeth died, England would once again have a Catholic ruler.'

'What happened to Mary?'

'There was a rebellion in Scotland, so she fled to England. She hoped her cousin would help her. Instead, Elizabeth put her in prison. Then, last year, she had her executed. That finally decided me to invade England.'

'Have you any other reasons for making war on the English, apart from religion?'

'Yes indeed. Columbus sailed to the West Indies in 1492. Since then, Spaniards have been exploring and making colonies in America. Most important of all, my people have discovered rich silver mines in Peru. It is the wealth from America which, more than anything, makes Spain strong. The English are jealous of our empire. Pirates like Drake are constantly attacking our settlements. They rob, burn and murder. The only way to stop them, is to conquer England. There is another reason, too. I rule over the Netherlands. But many of its people became Protestants. In 1568 they rebelled against me. My nephew, the Duke of Parma, is fighting them now. He has won several victories, but he has been unable to crush the rebels completely. One reason is that the English keep sending them help. I am sure I must conquer England, before I can reconquer the Netherlands.'

'What are your plans?'

'The Duke of Parma will lead the army of invasion from the Netherlands. But Parma has no warships. That means I must send an armada from Spain. It will sail up the English Channel. It will then escort Parma's men to England. If only they can land, they will make short work of the English. They may have a good fleet, but they have no army worthy of the name. Also, most English people are Catholics at heart. They will rebel against Elizabeth as soon as my men arrive.'

'We hear that Drake interrupted your plans by his attack on Cadiz last year. He was rude enough to say he had singed your beard.'

'Drake did burn some ships at Cadiz. But few of them were meant for the Armada. That is being prepared in Lisbon, which Drake did not dare attack. What Drake did do that alarmed us was to leave suddenly, and go after the treasure fleet. My admiral, the Marquis of Santa Cruz, sent thirty of our best ships to protect it. They did indeed save the treasure. But they were caught in a storm, and were badly damaged. It took us weeks to repair them. In the meantime, Santa Cruz died. I shall never find another admiral as good. Drake did us far more harm by leaving the coast of Spain than he did by coming here.'

'When, finally, your Armada does sail, do you think it will succeed?'

'I am sure of it. It will be going to do God's work, and God will give it victory.'

Note: Mary, Queen of Scots, was executed after there had been several Catholic plots. They were to assassinate Elizabeth and put Mary on the throne.

1 Why does Philip II want to invade England?

2 Whom had he hoped would become Queen, if he waited long enough?

3 Why did this woman come to England?

4 What did Philip decide he must do when she was executed?

5 What have the English been doing to the Spanish settlements in America?

6 According to Philip, what is the only way to stop them?

7 When did the Netherlands rebel against Philip II?

8 What is one reason why it has been impossible to crush the rebels?

9 Who will lead the army that is going to invade England?

10 Why must Philip send an armada (a fleet of warships) to help him?

11 What will the armada do, when it arrives?

12 Why does Philip think it will be easy for his army to conquer England once it has landed? (He gives two reasons.)

13 Why did Drake's raid on Cadiz not bother Philip a great deal?

14 In what way was Drake a serious nuisance to the Spaniards?

15 Who was Santa Cruz? What has happened to him? What problem does that leave Philip?

16 Why does Philip think his armada will be a success?

B The English and Spanish Fleets Compared

It is difficult to compare the English and Spanish fleets because there are not enough accurate facts and figures. However, we do have a few rough ideas.

It seems that there were exactly 130 ships of all kinds in the Armada. How many ships there were in the English fleet we do not know. Some writers say there were 160, but there are lists giving as many as 190. It is very likely, though, that the English out-numbered the Spaniards. Whether these extra numbers were any use to the English is another matter. Many of their vessels were little coasters that would not dare to take part in a battle.

In both fleets nearly all the fighting ships were armed merchantmen. They were pressed into service for the war. But both sides also had a number of true warships that had been built for fighting and nothing else. Those in the Armada were the King of Spain's galleons. There were twenty of these. Similarly, the true warships in the English fleet were the Queen's galleons. Eighteen of these were large and powerful. At one time it was thought that King Philip's galleons were bigger than Queen Elizabeth's. However, they were probably much the same size. In what we might call 'capital ships', then, the two fleets were roughly equal.

An important difference between the fleets was that the Spaniards carried a large number of soldiers, whereas the English did not. That

Figure 1 English Culverin (top) and Spanish Cannon

meant the Spaniards were anxious to grapple with the English and fight hand to hand. They knew they were nearly certain to take any ship they attacked in this way. The Spanish soldiers, however, would be quite useless, as long as the English ships kept a safe distance.

Now look at this table:

Guns of the English and Spanish Fleets

	Type of Gun	
	Cannon	Culverins
Range	2000 paces	2500 paces
Weight of Shot	24–60 pounds	9–18 pounds
English Guns	98	497
Spanish Guns	489	302

Note: The weight of shot shows the weight of the ball a gun could fire. For example, there were various sorts of cannon. The smallest fired a ball of 24 pounds, and the largest a ball of 60 pounds.

The largest cannon were 'ship smashers.' No vessel could stand being pounded with 50 or 60 pound shot for long.

1 Which fleet had the more cannon? Which had the more culverins?

2 How many of their guns could the English use, if the range was between 2000 and 2500 paces? How many could the Spaniards use at that range?

3 How many guns could the English use, if the range was less than 2000 paces? How many could the Spaniards use?

From the answers you have given to these questions, you will realise that the Spaniards wanted to fight at as close a range as possible. They could then use far more of their guns, including their deadly 'ship smashers.' The English, on the other hand, wanted to fight at a range of between 2000 and 2500 paces.

It is one thing, though, to decide on the range of your choice; it is quite another to keep it during a battle. The side that was going to do that, was the one with the better sailing ships. Thanks to John Hawkins, this was the English. Their ships were too nimble for the Spaniards and, most of the time, they were able to stay just where they liked to be. As we have seen, that was between 2000 and 2500 paces from their enemies.

It was unfortunate for the English, that the long range they wanted brought them two problems. In the first place, they found it very difficult to hit their targets. Secondly, most of their culverins were of the lighter kind, firing the 9 pound shot. At a big distance this shot simply rebounded from the tough oak sides of the Spanish galleons.

We can think of the Armada and the English fleet as two boxers in a ring. Both are about the same height and weight. The Spaniard packs a more powerful punch, but he is slow moving. The Englishman cannot punch as hard, but he is lighter on this feet, and can escape from his enemy whenever he wants. Who is likely to win in such a fight?

1 How many ships were there in the Armada?

2 How many were there in the English fleet? (Give the largest and the smallest estimates.)

3 Why were their extra numbers not much use to the English?

4 How many 'capital ships' were there in each fleet?

5 Why were the Spaniards anxious to grapple with the English?

6 At what range did the English want to fight? Why?

7 Why were they able to keep this range?

8 What were the two disadvantages of fighting at this long range?

9 How far, roughly, is 2000 paces, in modern measurements? (Sixteenth century people were smaller than us. One of their paces was about two thirds of a metre.)

C The Spaniards before the Fighting

In order to conquer England, Philip II needed an army and a fleet. He already had an army very close to England. It was in the Netherlands, fighting the Dutch. Its commander, an excellent general, was his nephew, the Duke of Parma. Philip decided that Parma should provide most of the soldiers for the invasion. Parma, however, had no warships, but only river barges to carry his men. That meant a fleet, or armada, would have to come from Spain. The main duty of the Armada would be to escort Parma's boats to England. But it was also to bring 6000 soldiers as reinforcements for Parma. Here are some of Philip's instructions to the commander of the Armada, the Duke of Medina Sidonia:

Document One

You will go straight to the English Channel, which you will sail up as far as Cape Margate. Here, you will join the Duke of Parma. You will protect his forces from the enemy while he crosses the Channel.

You will only fight, if this is the only way to make sure that the Duke of Parma can cross to England. If this can be done without fighting, for example by distracting the enemy, it would be better to do so. That way, you will keep your fleet intact.

Philip II to Medina Sidonia, 1 April, 1588

Note: There is no such place as Cape Margate.

1 Where is the Armada to sail?
2 What must it do when it arrives?
3 Why should the Armada try to avoid fighting while on its way?

Here are some more of Philip's orders to Medina Sidonia:

Document Two

All victories are the gift of God. We are going to do God's work, and we can rely on His help, unless, by our sins, we anger Him. You will therefore take good care that nothing is done to offend Him. Above all, there must be no swearing or blasphemy. You must punish offenders most severely, lest God should punish us all.

Philip II to Medina Sidonia, 1 April, 1588

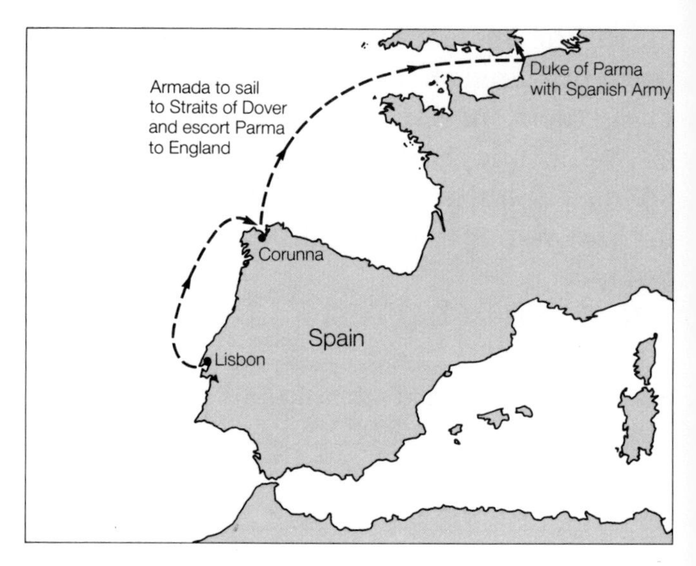

Figure 1 The Spanish Plan of Invasion

Note: 'blasphemy' – insulting God

1 According to Philip II, who will help the Spaniards?
2 What must the men in the Armada avoid doing?
3 Why must those who disobey be punished severely?

The man who had been chosen, originally, to lead the Armada, was a splendid seaman, the Marquis of Santa Cruz. However, he died early in 1588, just a week before the Armada was due to sail. Philip II had to look for another commander. The main problem was to find someone so important that everyone in the fleet would be willing to obey him. The high ranking Spanish officers were all nobles. They were very proud and there were few people from whom they would take orders. Accordingly, Philip chose as his commander-in-chief one of the greatest men in Spain, the Duke of Medina Sidonia. When he heard the news of his appointment, Medina Sidonia sent this letter to the King's secretary:

Document Three

I am not well at sea, for I know from the few

times I have been afloat that I soon become sea-sick. Besides, as you know, I am short of money. I owe 900,000 ducats, and I have not a single penny I can spend on the expedition. Moreover, the force is so great and its task so important, that it would not be right for someone like me to take charge of it. I know nothing of seafaring or war at sea. Besides all this, I know nothing about the Armada, of the men who are in it, or of the plans the Marquis of Santa Cruz has been making for years past. I should be working in the dark and should have to be guided by others, without knowing whether their advice was good or bad, or whether they were trying to deceive me.

I have no doubt that his Majesty, in his kindness, will not give me a task at which I would certainly fail. For I do not understand it, I know nothing about it, I have no money to spend on it, and I am unfit to go to sea.

Medina Sidonia to Juan d'Idiaquez, 16 February 1588

1 What happens to Medina Sidonia when he goes to sea?
2 Why is he unable to pay anything towards the cost of the Armada?
3 What does he know about war at sea?
4 What does he know about the Armada?
5 What is he afraid will happen, if he is put in charge?
6 Was Philip II wise to choose Medina Sidonia, do you think?

The Armada finally sailed from Lisbon at the end of May. It was due to go to Corunna to take on water, and some of the ships arrived there on June 19th. The rest were caught in a great storm. They were scattered, and many were badly damaged. Medina Sidonia wrote to the King from Corunna:

Document Four

When your Majesty ordered me to take command of this Armada, I gave your Majesty many reasons why I should not do so. This was not because I wanted to refuse. But I realised we were attacking a country so powerful, and so warmly helped by its neighbours, that we

Figure 2 The Duke of Medina Sidonia

would need a much larger force than your Majesty had gathered at Lisbon.

None the less, your Majesty ordered me to sail, which I did. We have now arrived at this port badly damaged. Many of our largest ships are still missing. On the ships that are here, many of the men are sick, and their numbers will grow because of the bad provisions. Not only are they very bad, but they are so short that they cannot last for more than two months. From this your Majesty may judge whether we should continue with the voyage.

I remember how great an army your Majesty collected to conquer Portugal, which is our neighbour, and many of whose people were on your side. Well, Sire, how do you suppose we can attack so powerful a country as England with the force we now have?

All our difficulties could be avoided by making an honourable peace with the enemy.

Medina Sidonia to Philip II, 24 June 1588

1 According to Medina Sidonia, why had he been unwilling to take charge of the Armada?

2 Was this one of the reasons he, in fact, gave? (See *Document Three*.)
3 What are some of the things that have gone wrong with the Armada?
4 What does Medina Sidonia want the King to do, rather than go on with the invasion?

It was not only storms and the English that worried the Duke. As you saw in the last document, he mentions supplies going bad. The Venetian ambassador in Madrid wrote:

Document Five
The Duke of Medina Sidonia says that the provisions for the Armada are already almost all eaten or gone bad. He has had to throw overboard great quantities of biscuits, cheese and salt meat, which were quite rotten. The guilty contractors who supplied the food are to be put on trial.
Hieronomino Lippomano to the Doge, 7 July 1588

Figure 3 Spanish Army Camp

1 What food has been thrown away?
2 What is to happen to the contractors who supplied it?

While he was in Corunna, Medina Sidonia was supposed to pick up some soldiers from Galicia, in North-West Spain. This is what he told the King about them:

Document Six
The 400 Galician soldiers sent by the Count of Lemos, are useless. They are nearly all married and have large families. In fact, they are old men, unfit for service. Their wives have been coming in weeping so much that my conscience will not let me take the men. The captains will have nothing to do with them. Obviously, they would simply die on board the ships. Some are already more dead than alive. Not one of them knows what an arquebus is, or any other weapon. Under the circumstances, I thought it best to send them all home.
Medina Sidonia to Philip II, 19 July 1588

Note: 'arquebus' – early type of musket

1 What are some of the things that are wrong with the Galician soldiers?
2 What is Medina Sidonia afraid will happen to them, if he takes them to sea?
3 What has he decided to do with them?

Do not imagine that all Spanish soldiers were like these men from Galicia. In those days, the Spanish regular army was the best in Europe. *Document Six* is interesting because it shows the kind of man one Spanish nobleman was willing to spare from his estates.

The other commander on whom Philip was counting was the Duke of Parma. Here are some letters which he wrote to the King:

Document Seven
a. The infantry are all ready, and all together, but the cavalry are scattered. Since there was no food for them here, I had to send them to

Figure 4 Parma's Army

Hainault and Tournai.

I am doing my best to keep the troops in good spirits, but the infantry is no more than 18,000 men. Even if they give me 6000 men from the Armada, my force will still be weak. Sickness will reduce it even more.

b. I see that the Duke of Medina Sidonia is to give me 6000 Spaniards. I am sorry that your Majesty is unable to let me have any more. The Spaniards must be our right arm, and we have very few of them here, though the experienced soldiers among them are the best in the world. We are short of good pilots and even of seamen. If the crossing was a long one, we could not attempt it.

c. I am in despair for lack of money, since your Majesty has ordered that the 670,000 ducats I was expecting should be spent on the Armada.
Duke of Parma to Philip II, April–June 1588

Note: Parma was planning to sail from Dunkirk.

1 What has Parma done with his cavalry? Why?
2 What does Parma feel about the size of his army?
3 What does Parma feel about the number of soldiers Medina Sidonia is bringing?
4 What soldiers is Parma short of?
5 What other men is he short of?
6 According to Parma, what has happened to the money he was expecting?

Philip suggested that when the Armada drew near to Dunkirk, Parma's men should sail out to meet it. Parma wrote to the King:

Document Eight

With the small, flat bottomed boats built for rivers and not for the sea, I must take the shortest passage to England. Even when we are protected, and the enemy driven from the Channel, it will be a great mercy from God, if we reach land in these vessels. I cannot go out of my way to meet the Armada. If I did so, and we met any English or Dutch ships, they would destroy us easily. Neither the courage of our men, nor anything we might do could save us.
Duke of Parma to Philip II, 22 June 1588

1 What shape are Parma's boats? What were they built for?
2 Why must Parma take the shortest possible route to England?
3 What does he fear might happen, if he went out of his way to meet the Armada?

D The English before the Fighting

The English knew perfectly well that the Spaniards were preparing the Armada. What they did not know was where or when the Spaniards would attack. The men in the English fleet hated waiting and wondering. The English admiral, Lord Howard of Effingham, wrote to Walsingham, one of the Queen's ministers:

Document One

The opinion of Sir Francis Drake, Mr. Hawkins, Mr. Frobisher and others of great experience, is that the surest way to meet with the Spanish fleet is upon their own coast, or any harbour of their own, and there to defeat them. I agree with them. But I believe they mean to linger on their own coasts until they hear we have spent our victuals. Therefore we must attack them before that happens.

Howard to Walsingham, 24 June 1588

Note: 'spent our victuals' – eaten all our food

1. What men has Howard consulted?
2. Where do they say it would be best to attack the Spaniards?
3. Where does Howard think the Spaniards mean to wait? Why?

Figure 1 English Warship, the *Golden Lion*.

In fact, the government forbade Howard to go far from England. He wrote to Walsingham, 'I must and will obey.' But he added, sarcastically, 'I am glad there be people in London who are able to judge what is fit for us to do, better than we are here.'

As you saw in Document One, Howard was worried about a shortage of food. He wrote many letters to the government, like this one he sent from Plymouth:

Document Two
Sir, I will never again come to such a place as this without bringing my victuals with me, and not trust to careless men behind me. We came away with hardly a month's victuals. It would have been little enough to have gone to Flushing. We think it wonderful how we keep our men from running away, for they all know how long our victuals will last. But I thank God that, as yet, we are not troubled with mutinies. For I see men kindly handled will bear want and run through fire and water.

I doubt not but if this month's victuals come unto us from London, we will make it to serve us very near three months. Sir, I pray you to send here some money for the soldiers and sailors who have done their duty very well until now.
Howard to Walsingham, 23 June 1588

1 How long will the food last?
2 What is Howard afraid the men might do? Has this, in fact, happened?
3 What does Howard promise to do, if he can have a month's supply of food? (He is, of course, exaggerating.)
4 What does Howard ask for, as well as food?

Sailors ate in groups, and each group was called a 'mess.' Normally, there were four men in a mess. To make the food go further, Howard ordered that there should be six men in every mess. They would, of course, only draw enough rations for four.

It was not only food and pay which the fleet lacked. Drake wrote to the government:

Document Three
The powder and shot for our great guns in Her Majesty's ships is but enough for one and a half day's fighting. Good my Lords, I beg you to consider deeply of this, for it means that we shall lose all.
Drake to the Council, 30 March 1588

1 According to Drake, how much ammunition does the fleet have?
2 What is Drake afraid will happen, as a result?

By far the most important ships in the English fleet were the ones that belonged to the Queen. But there were not nearly enough of them. To make up the numbers, the government asked all the seaside towns to send armed merchant ships. This was the reply that came from Poole:

Document Four
Our obedient duties unto your Honours in most humble wise remembered. Your Honours' letters we have received; the contents whereof is that Her Majesty doth understand that there are a very good number of very good ships belonging to this town and that we should make choice of one ship of 60 tons and one pinnace, to be furnished for two months. Our humble petition unto your good Lordships now is, that it may please you to consider the great poverty of this poor town, by reason of want of trade, loss at sea, and by pirates that do continually lie at Studland Bay, being at the mouth of this harbour. And lately having been at great charge in building defences against the enemy, we are quite unable to perform your Lordships' commandment to set forth a ship and a pinnace.
Mayor and Aldermen of Poole to the Council, 5 April 1588

Notes: All Poole had done in the way of building defences was to repair a small fort on Brownsea Island.

The people of Poole, including the Mayor, were often in league with pirates.

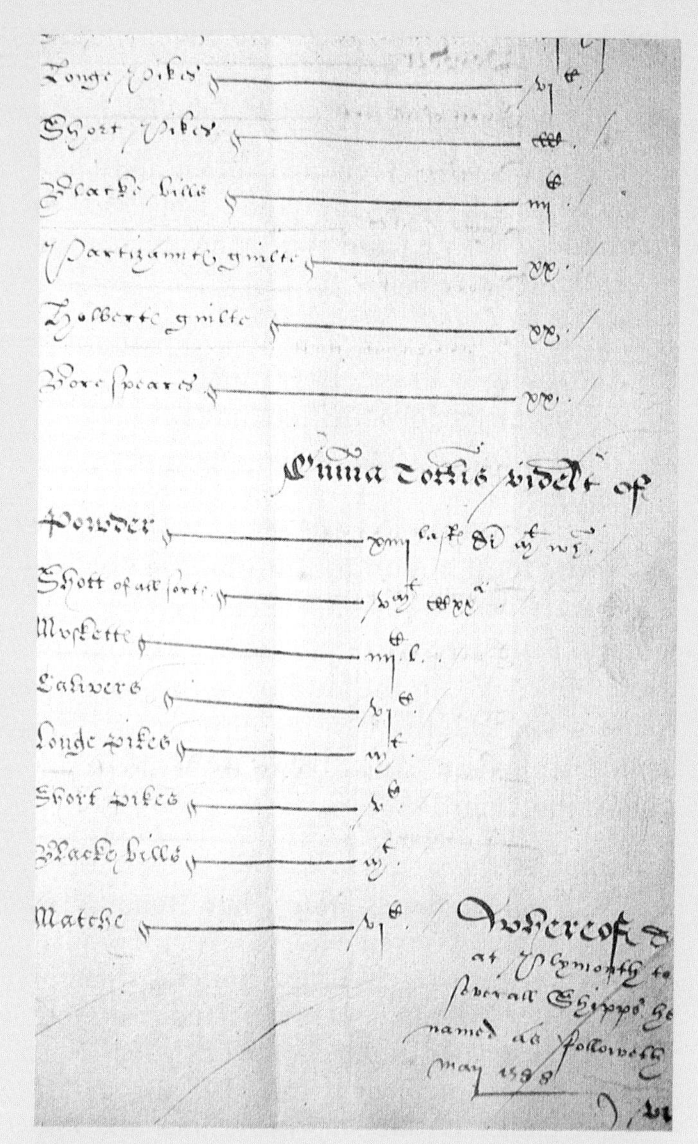
Longe pikes
Short pikes
Blacke bills
Partizannes gilte
Holberte gilte
Bore speares
Summa totis videl' of
Powder
Shott of all sortes
Muskette
Calivers
Longe pikes
Short pikes
Blacke bills
Matche
Whereof at Plymouth to serve all Shipps he named as followeth
May 1588

Figure 2 Part of an Inventory of Ammunition and Weapons in the English Fleet

1 What ships has Poole been asked to provide?

2 According to the Mayor and Aldermen:

- **a** Why is Poole a poor town?
- **b** What big expense has the town had?
- **c** What is the town unable to do as a result?

Several other towns answered in much the same way as Poole. Many, though, did provide ships, especially London. London sent thirty vessels in all, some of them as powerful as the ones in the Royal Navy.

There were certain problems which the English did not have. Here are extracts from two of Howard's letters:

Document Five

a. The *Elizabeth Bonaventure* came aground on a sand bar. The next tide, by the goodness of God and great labour we brought her off. In all this time there never came a spoonful of water into her. My Lord, except a ship had been made of iron, it were unpossible to do as she has done. It may be well and truly said there never was nor is in the world a stronger ship than she is.

b. May it please God to continue her Majesty's ships as strong unto the end of the war, as they have done until now. Her Majesty may be sure she has the strongest ships that any prince in Christendom has.

Howard to Burghley, 9 March and 14 June 1588

1 According to Howard, what good quality do the Queen's ships have?

Drake wrote to the Queen:

Document Six

I have not in my lifetime known better men, and possessed with braver minds than your Majesty's people who are here gathered together for the finishing of this great piece of work. We are all certain that God, the giver of all victories, will in mercy look upon your most excellent Majesty and us, your poor subjects, who, for the defence of your Majesty, our religion, and native country, have resolutely vowed to risk our lives.

Drake to the Queen, 13 April 1588

1 What does Drake feel about the men in the English fleet?

2 According to Drake, whose side is God on?

Further Work

1 Compare the problems that the Spaniards and the English had before the fighting began. In what ways were these problems similar?

2 Which side seems to you the more confident of winning? Give your reasons for your answer.

E The Fighting in the English Channel

The Armada arrived off the Lizard on July 29th. It caught the English in Plymouth. Moreover, it was going to be very difficult for them to come out, since the wind was south-west. But they towed their ships out of Plymouth harbour, and then managed to sail the other side of the Spaniards. The path they followed is shown by the zig-zag line on the map. (Figure 1.) The English had now 'got the wind' of their enemies. It was a great advantage, for it meant they could attack whenever, or wherever they wanted.

Probably, though, Medina Sidonia was not too worried about what had happened. Just before he had left Lisbon, he had written to the King:

Document One

If I do not find the enemy in my way, I will not seek him, but will press on to join the Duke of Parma. If Drake lets me pass on and then comes out and attacks me, I have taken every care. This will be seen from the formation I have decided to use. Either of its two horns will be able to deal with the enemy's fleet.

Medina Sidonia to Philip II, 28 May 1588

To understand what Medina Sidonia meant you need to look at Figure 1. The Spanish fleet is in the shape of a half moon. The most powerful of the fighting ships make up the horns of the moon. The weaker ships, such as the ones carrying troops and supplies, are in the centre. The English are more or less bound to attack the powerful Spanish ships on the horns. If they make for the Spanish centre, what will the horns do?

On July 31st. the English attacked. Here are three English accounts of this, the first battle:

Document Two

a. At nine of the clock we gave them fight, which continued until one. In this fight we made some of them bear room to stop their leaks. None the less, we dared not go in among them, their fleet being so strong.

Howard to Walsingham, 31 July 1588

b. On the 31st. we had them in chase. Coming up to them, there was some shot between some of our fleet and some of them. As far as

Figure 1 The Armada off the Coast of Devon. The map suggests that Howard attacked the centre of the Spanish fleet. This he did not do. Why do you think the map is inaccurate?

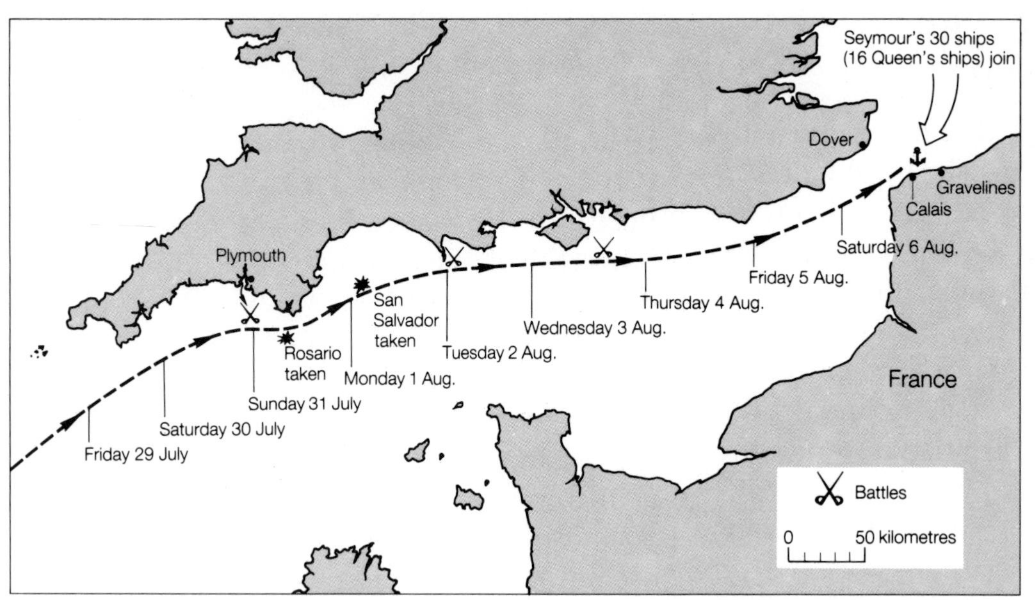

Figure 2 Route taken up the Channel by the Armada Philip II ordered the Armada to sail near the coast of England, because he believed it was less dangerous for shipping than the coast of France. The English thought the Spaniards were trying to land, but that they had prevented them. How long did it take the Spaniards to sail up the Channel?

we can see, they are determined to sell their lives with blows.
Sir Francis Drake to Lord Henry Seymour, 31 July 1588

c. The majesty of the enemy's fleet, and the good order they kept did cause our first attack to be coldly done.
Henry Whyte to Walsingham, 8 August 1588

Note: 'bear room' – sail away

1 According to Howard, how long did the fight last?
2 What shows that the English did not attack very strongly?
3 What reason does Henry Whyte give for this?
4 What shows that the Spaniards fought bravely?

Here is Medina Sidonia's account:

Document Three
Our Armada placed itself in order of battle, and the flagship hoisted the royal standard. The enemy's fleet fell on our rear, which was in the charge of Admiral Juan Martinez de Recalde. He stood fast. The enemy did not close, but attacked him with heavy gunfire from a distance. His ship's rigging was much damaged, and her foremast was struck by two great shot. Supporting Juan Martinez de Recalde were Don Diego de Pimental and Don Diego Enriquez. The flagship struck her topsail and waited for the rear to join the main body of the fleet. At this, the enemy drew off and I gathered my fleet together. I was unable to do anything more because the enemy's ships were very swift and nimble, so that they did with them whatever they wanted.
Medina Sidonia to Philip II, 21 August 1588

Note: 'rear' – Medina Sidonia means the southern horn of the Armada.

1 Which part of the Spanish fleet did the English attack?
2 Where was Recalde's ship damaged? Would this damage have been difficult to repair, do you think?
3 Medina Sidonia had expected that the English would fight from a distance. Was this what happened?
4 Medina Sidonia would have liked to close with the English and then grapple and board them. Why were the Spaniards unable to do this?

Here are more extracts from Medina Sidonia's report. They describe things that happened during later battles in the Channel:

Document Four
a. *August 2nd* Captain Bertendona very bravely attacked their flagship, offering to board her. But as he came near her, she made off, and

stood out to sea

b. Our flagship, seeing the enemy's flagship in the lead, turned towards her and lowered her topsails. The enemy's flagship, and all the fleet passed her, shooting at her, ship by ship. She, on her part, fired her guns very well and fast and, as a result, half the enemy's fleet did not come near, but shot at her from afar.

c. *August 4th* The enemy's flagship and other great ships attacked our flagship. They came closer than the first day, firing their big guns from the lower deck, and killed some of our soldiers. There came to the aid of our flagship, three of our own great ships. At this, the enemy withdrew. The enemy's flagship was so damaged in the fight that now she was towed by eleven of the enemy's long boats. Our flagship and the rest of the ships were gaining on her so much that it seemed certain we would succeed in boarding them, which was the only way to victory. But at this moment the wind freshened in favour of the enemy's flagship and she began to slip away. Meanwhile, the wind had shifted to the south-west. Seeing that an attack was now useless, I ordered our flagship to go on her way. The rest of the armada followed in very good order. The enemy remained a long way astern.

Medina Sidonia to Philip II, 21 August 1588

1 In the first and third of these extracts, Medina Sidonia says that the Spaniards tried to board the English. What did the English do whenever the Spaniards came near?

2 What did half the English fleet not do in their attack on the Spanish flagship on August 2nd? (Extract **b.**) What did the English ships do instead?

3 In what sort of order was the Armada at the end of August 4th.?

During the fighting, the Armada kept its formation well. An English officer wrote, 'They do keep such excellent good order in their fight, that unless God works some miracle, we shall have hard fighting for some days.' We can discover one reason for this good order in Medina Sidonia's report:

Document Five

I called to me all the sergeant majors, and told them to visit all the ships in the fleet. They carried with them written orders giving each ship the place it should take. Further, I told them that if any ship left its place, they should at once hang its captain. So that they could carry out that order, they took with them the provost marshals and their hangmen.

Medina Sidonia to Philip II, 21 August 1588

1 What is to happen to any Spanish captain who allows his ship to leave its place?

After August 4th. there was no more serious fighting in the Channel. On August 6th. the Armada dropped anchor off Calais.

The English were pleased with what had happened so far. An English officer, Richard Thomson, wrote, 'We have so daily pursued them at the heels that they never had the chance to stop in any place along our English coast.'

Medina Sidonia must have seen things differently. His orders were to sail the length of the English Channel, and then escort Parma's troops to England. The first of these orders he had obeyed, and obeyed well. He had sailed along the enemy coast for nine days, and had fought several battles. Now, he was a few miles from Parma's army, with his fleet still intact and in good order. He was disappointed that he had not captured or destroyed any English ships. On the other hand, the English had fired their guns at such long range that they had done no serious damage.

The Armada's journey up the Channel, followed by the English, was a bit like a herd of well-behaved bulls going along a road with a pack of dogs snapping at its heels. Once in a while the bulls turn to fight. Then the dogs, being faster, escape quite easily. Neither the dogs nor the bulls are badly hurt, but the bulls go exactly where they want. All the time the dogs think the bulls are running away!

F The Loss of the *Rosario*

While they were in the Channel, the Spaniards had accidents that cost them two of their largest ships. One of them blew up. The other, the *Rosario*, broke her foremast, which meant she could not keep up with the rest of the Armada. Later, her captain, Don Pedro de Valdes, wrote to the King:

Document One

I twice sent word to the Duke (of Medina Sidonia), begging him to send a ship to tow me. But although he might easily have helped me, yet he would not do it. Instead, he called the fleet together and went on his way. The enemy was but a quarter of a league from me, and reached me at the end of the day. Some ships attacked me, but I defended myself all that night. I still hoped the Duke would send me some help.

Don Pedro Valdes to Philip II, 31 August 1588

1 What did Valdes ask the Duke to do?
2 What did Medina Sidonia do instead?
3 How does Valdes feel about Medina Sidonia, do you think?

This is Medina Sidonia's account:

Document Two

The foremast of Don Pedro's ship broke and fell on the main yard. I turned my ship to help him, and tried to pass him a cable. But although we did all we could, the weather and the sea prevented us. General Diego Flores told me that if I waited for Don Pedro, it would not be possible for the fleet to see me, because they were so far ahead. Without doubt, by morning, half the fleet would be missing. Since the enemy was so near, he would be certain to defeat us. Upon hearing this, I ordered Captain Ojeda to take Don Pedro's ship in tow, and remove her men. But neither the one nor the other was possible, owing to the heavy sea, the darkness and the weather.

I went on my way and rejoined the fleet, taking care to keep it together for whatever might happen the following day.

Medina Sidonia to Philip II, 21 August 1588

1 According to Medina Sidonia, how did he try to help Don Pedro de Valdes? Why did he fail?
2 What did Diego Flores say would happen if Medina Sidonia waited for Don Pedro?
3 What was Captain Ojeda ordered to do? Why did he fail?
4 What did Medina Sidonia feel he must do at all costs? (See last sentence.)
5 Do you think Diego Flores's advice to the Duke was sound?

The morning after the accident, Don Pedro's crippled ship was captured by Drake. How that happened is rather curious.

The same evening that Don Pedro was left behind by the Armada, the English admiral, Howard of Effingham, ordered Sir Francis Drake to set the watch for the night. That meant Drake had to lead the English fleet. He was supposed to light his stern lanterns, so that the other ships could follow him. Howard describes what happened:

Document Three

I appointed Sir Francis Drake to set the watch that night. But he left the watch to pursue certain hulks which were seen very late in the evening. The fleet, not seeing his light, lingered behind, not knowing whom to follow. Only my ship, with the *Bear* and the *Mary Rose*, pursued the enemy all night within culverin shot. My own fleet was so far behind that, the next morning, the nearest could hardly be seen at half mast high, and very many out of sight. Sailing as fast as they could, they did not overtake me before it was very late in the evening.

Howard to the Privy Council, August 1588

Note: 'hulk' – merchant ship

1 According to Howard, why did Drake leave his watch?
2 What was the fleet unable to see, as a result? What did most of it do?
3 Why was Howard in great danger the next morning?
4 How long was it before the English fleet was together again?

Figure 1 The capture of the *Rosario* This picture was not meant to show distances accurately. The *Rosario* is being attacked in the bottom left hand corner.

Soon after the Armada had been defeated, one of Drake's men, Matthew Starke, was questioned by Sir Martin Frobisher. Frobisher hated Drake. This was how the interview went:

Document Four

FROBISHER: Did you see Don Pedro's ship during the night?
STARKE: No.
FROBISHER: You lie. She was seen by the whole fleet.
STARKE: Not any man in our ship saw her until morning, when we were within two or three cable lengths of her.
FROBISHER: Ay, marry, you were within two or three cable lengths all night.
STARKE: No, for we carried a good sail all night.
FROBISHER: Why did you leave the fleet?
STARKE: We saw three or four hulks, and we went to find out what they were.
FROBISHER: Drake was told to carry a light all that night. We looked for that light, but there was no light to be seen. In the morning, when we should have attacked the Spaniards, there were not more than five or six ships with our Admiral. The reason was, that we did not see Drake's light.

Deposition of Matthew Starke, 11 August 1588

1 According to Frobisher, where was Drake all night?
2 According to Starke, why did Drake leave the fleet?
3 According to Frobisher:
  a. What was the fleet looking for, in vain, all night?
  b. What should the English have done in the morning?
  c. Why did they not do so?
  d. Who was to blame?

It seems that Frobisher also said, 'Drake thinks he can cheat us of our share of 15,000 ducats. But we will have our shares, or I will make him spend the best blood in his belly.'

The 15,000 ducats were money that was found on the *Rosario*. As she was Drake's prize, he shared this money with his crew.

No action was taken against Drake, and for most people he was still a hero. What would have happened to any Spanish captain who behaved as he did? (See *Document Five*, page 63)

G The Armada at Calais

As you have already seen, the Armada arrived off Calais on August 6th. Calais is only 25 miles from Dunkirk, where the Duke of Parma was supposed to be ready and waiting to cross the Channel.

Medina Sidonia had sent messages to Parma from time, telling him of the Armada's progress. Parma had not replied. Then, the day after the Armada reached Calais, a messenger arrived. He had been sent, not by Parma, but by one of Medina Sidonia's own men. Medina Sidonia said:

> *Document One*
> On Sunday night the Secretary Arceo sent me a messenger from Dunkirk. He told me the Duke of Parma had not arrived there, and that the munitions were not being embarked. He said he thought it would be impossible for everything to be ready in less than a fortnight.
> *Medina Sidonia to Philip II*, 21 August 1588

1 How long does Arceo think it will be before Parma is ready?

Meanwhile, the English had no intention of leaving the Spaniards in peace. An officer on one of the London ships describes what happened:

> *Document Two*
> My Lord Admiral ordered certain small ships to be fired on Sunday about twelve of the clock at night, and let drive with the tide amongst the Spaniards. This, God be thanked, has turned to our great good. It caused the Spaniards to let slip their anchors and, in confusion, to drive upon one another. They were not only put from their roadstead where they meant to wait for the Duke of Parma, but did much hurt to one another.
> *Richard Tomson to Walsingham*, 9 August 1588

1 How did the English attack the Spaniards?

2 According to Tomson, what did the Spaniards do when they were attacked?

This is Medina Sidonia's account:

> *Document Three*
> On Sunday at sunset, the enemy moved nearer to the land, which made us suppose they were going to use fireships. I ordered all the ships to be on their guard. At midnight, two fires were seen in the English fleet, which increased to

Figure 1 The Fireships launched against the Armada The ship with oars is a galleas, perhaps the *San Lorenzo*.

eight. Suddenly, eight ships with sail set, and driven with wind and tide came straight towards us, all burning fiercely. Fearing they might contain explosion machines, I gave order to weigh anchor. When the fireships had passed by, I meant to return to the same position. My flagship and some other ships that were near her did anchor. But the current was so strong that it swept the rest of the Armada far away. They did not see us, and were driven off as far as Dunkirk.

Meanwhile, the galleass *San Lorenzo* collided with the *San Juan de Sicilia* and damaged herself so badly that she had to run aground.
Medina Sidonia to Philip II, 21 August 1588

Note: A fireship was filled with anything that would burn and any barrels of gunpowder that could be spared. Also, its guns were loaded. Its crew pointed it towards the enemy, and lashed its rudder. When it was well under way, they took to their boats. The last man to leave the ship threw a blazing torch into the hold.
'galleas' – ship with oars as well as sails

1. What made the Spaniards suspect that the English were going to use fireships?
2. How many fireships did the English send?
3. What was Medina Sidonia afraid the fireships might contain?
4. What did he order the Armada to do?
5. What did he intend to do, when the fireships had passed by?
6. Why did most of the Armada not do so?
7. What happened to the *San Lorenzo*?

In the days of wooden ships, sailors were very scared of fire. But it is hard to understand why such a well disciplined force as the Armada panicked as badly as it did. Possibly there is a clue in Medina Sidonia's mention of 'explosion machines.' An Italian called Giambelli had invented a powerful mine for use in fireships. It went off with an enormous explosion, causing damage over a wide area. Giambelli's fireships were so deadly that they were called 'hell burners'. In 1588, Giambelli

Figure 2 The Destruction of Parma's Bridge at Antwerp, 1585
Parma had built this bridge across the Schelde, to blockade Antwerp. One of Giambelli's 'hell burners' was sailed against it and exploded. It blew a great gap in the bridge and killed 800 Spaniards. After that, the Spaniards were very wary of fireships.

was in London, working for the English. The men on the Armada, therefore, had every reason to think that the fireships coming towards them were 'hell burners'. This would explain why they fled in some disorder. In fact, Howard's fireships were quite ordinary ones. They did not set fire to any Spanish ship, and burnt out harmlessly on the shore. By then, though, the Armada was scattered.

As you saw, the galleass *San Lorenzo* had been damaged and run aground at Calais. Here was another rich prize, and this time it was the Lord Admiral of England, Howard of Effingham, who neglected his duty for plunder. He ordered the fleet to chase the Spaniards, while he stayed behind with his flagship to loot her. He sent his men in boats, to board her.

Howard, though, was not as lucky as Drake. Calais was a French town, and France was neutral in the war. The governor, Monsieur de Gourdan, made the Spaniards welcome when they arrived. He also made the English welcome when they arrived in their turn. This lasted until some English sailors started robbing Frenchmen. Gourdan then turned his guns on the English boats, and they had to abandon the *San Lorenzo*.

H The Battle of Gravelines

On the morning of August 8th., which was the day after it left Calais, the Armada was near Gravelines. Here, the English attacked it, and there followed the most important battle of the campaign. This is Medina Sidonia's account of it:

> *Document One*
> The enemy attacked with great shooting of guns, coming within musket-shot. This went on without stopping from daybreak. Our ships resisted the enemy as bravely as possible. Many of them were badly damaged, so that they were unable to fight any more. Many ran out of ammunition for their guns.
>
> Some of our ships came near to boarding the enemy, yet they could not grapple with them. They fought with their big guns. Our men defended themselves with musket fire, the distance being very small.
>
> I heard the musket fire but, because of the smoke, could not see from the topmast what it was, except that a few of our ships were surrounded by the enemy, and that their whole fleet was attacking them. Accordingly, I took my ship to help them. She was badly holed on the water line, and leaking fast, while her rigging was much torn. None the less, when the enemy saw her approach, they left the ships they were attacking. The three that had been most hotly engaged with the enemy had all suffered heavy damage and were useless. Only one of them was able to follow us. I collected my fleet, and the enemy did the same.
> *Medina Sidonia to Philip II,* 21 August 1588

1 During the fighting in the Channel, the English had been careful to fight at long range. At Gravelines, they fought at short range. What happened to several Spanish ships, as a result?

2 What did the English still prevent the Spaniards from doing? (See second paragraph.)

Medina Sidonia says what happened the following day:

> *Document Two*
> At daybreak, the enemy was seen about two miles away. He kept his distance, seeing our

Figure 1 The Battle of Gravelines This is a fanciful picture by someone who did not see the battle, but it shows all the confusion.

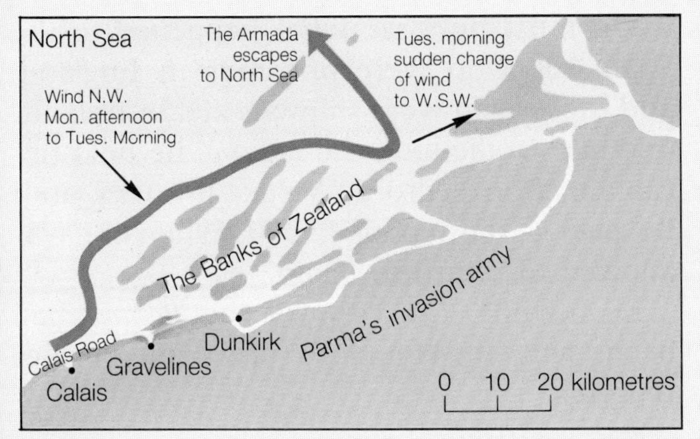

Figure 2 Course followed by the Armada during the Battle of Gravelines

Armada must be lost. The pilots who knew the coast, told me it was impossible to save a single ship of the Armada. Since the wind was in the North-West, they would all be driven onto the banks of Zeeland. God alone could prevent it. Being in this danger, with nothing we could do, and in six and a half fathoms of water, God was pleased to change the wind to West-South-West. At this, our fleet sailed towards the North without hurt to any ship.
Medina Sidonia to Philip II, 21 August 1588

1 According to the pilots, what was the North-West wind going to do to the Armada? Who alone could prevent this?
2 Why was the Armada saved?

It seems strange that the English did not attack the Spaniards when they were in such trouble. An English officer, Henry Whyte, explains why. He said of the Battle of Gravelines:

Document Three
We made a very strong attack, which continued some nine hours. Truly, if we had had shot and powder enough to have given them two attacks more, we should have totally destroyed them. By this your Honour may see how our parsimony at home has robbed us of the greatest victory that ever our navy might have had at sea.
Henry Whyte to Walsingham, 18 August 1588

Note: 'parsimony' – being mean

1 Why were the English unable to attack again after the Battle of Gravelines?
2 According to Henry Whyte, what would have happened if they had made two more attacks?
3 What was to blame for the failure?

When the Armada was safely away from the sandbanks, Medina Sidonia held a council of war. The fleet was out of ammunition, many ships were badly damaged, and Parma was still not ready. Accordingly, it was decided to sail for Spain, round the north of Scotland.

The English followed the Spaniards as far as the Firth of Forth. They then turned for home.

A curious thing about the Battle of Gravelines is that the English fought at close range. None of their accounts explains why, so we must look for clues.

There is one clue in Medina Sidonia's description of the battle. He says that many of his ships were out of ammunition, and speaks of his own men fighting with muskets, while the English used their big guns. Possibly, the English realised the Spaniards did not have enough gunpowder for their 'ship smashers' and closed the range to do more damage with their own guns.

Another clue is that the Battle of Gravelines was confused. The English accounts speak of fierce fighting, but give no clear idea of what happened. As for Medina Sidonia, we have his own description of how he climbed to his topmast and peered in vain through the smoke. All he did see was a small group of his own ships surrounded by large numbers of the English. Since the battle was confused, it would seem that the Spaniards were still scattered following their flight from Calais. That would have given the English the chance to concentrate on isolated Spanish ships. They would have risked closing the range with an enemy they outnumbered.

Much of this is guesswork, but it is clear that the English did close the range at Gravelines, and that they badly damaged numbers of the enemy as a result.

I The Spaniards after the Fighting

When the English turned back, the Armada sailed round the North of Scotland. In the Atlantic it ran into heavy storms. These were too much for many of the ships, especially those that had been damaged by the English. Probably, no more than eight ships had been lost in the fighting, but now 20 were wrecked on the coast of Ireland, and another 35 vanished, we know not how. Of the 130 ships that had left Spain, 63 did not return.

Medina Sidonia and his officers were worried about what the King might do. But Philip said the disaster was the will of God, and only one man was punished. This was Diego Flores, who spent 15 months in prison for advising Medina Sidonia to abandon the *Rosario*.

We must now see what happened to the Spaniards who were prisoners in England, and those who were shipwrecked in Ireland.

When Drake took the *Rosario*, he held her captain, Don Pedro de Valdes prisoner until he paid a ransom of £3000, when he was allowed to return to Spain.

Meanwhile, the crew of the *Rosario* had been sent to Plymouth. Two magistrates reported:

Document One

And touching the said prisoners, being in number 397, we have put 226 in our Bridewell. Watching and guarding the prisoners and taking victuals unto them was very burdensome unto our people in this time of harvest. Therefore, we have placed the remainder aboard the Spanish ship to live upon such victuals as do remain in the said ship. These are very little and bad, their fish stinking and their

Figure 1 Course followed by retreating Armada

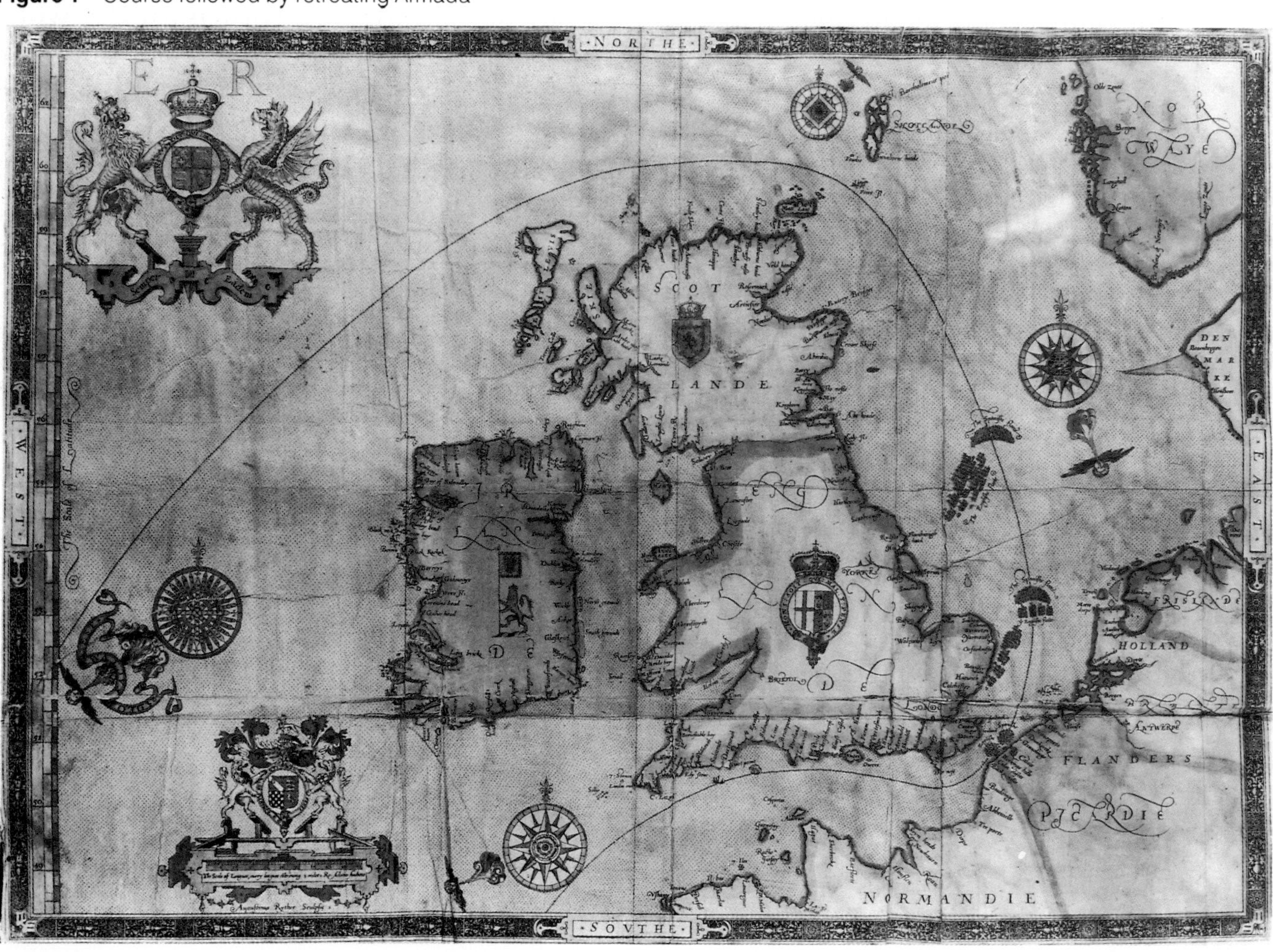

bread full of worms, and of so small a quantity as will last them a very small time.
John Gilbert and George Carey to the Council

Note: 'Bridewell' – prison for vagabonds

1 How are the Spaniards being a burden to the people?
2 Where are they being held?

Eventually, these men were sent back to Spain. They were lucky compared with those who were driven ashore in Ireland. The Governor of Connaught in South-West Ireland reported:

Document Two
Their loss upon this coast was twelve ships which we know of, and some two or three more thought to be sunk out at sea. The men of these ships did all perish in the sea, save 1100 or more which we put to the sword. Among them were some fifty gentlemen of quality, whom I spared from the sword till order might be had from the Lord Deputy how to proceed against them. I had orders sent me to see them executed.

Some five or six Dutch boys and young men I spared. I did this because they were pressed into the fleet against their wills. But the Lord Deputy caused them to be executed.
Sir Richard Bingham to the Queen, 2 December, 1588

Note: The Lord Deputy was the man who ruled Ireland for the Queen. In 1588 he was Sir William Fitzwilliam.

1 What happened to the Spaniards who escaped drowning?
2 Which Spaniards did Bingham spare? Why did he do that, do you suppose? (Remember what happened to Don Pedro de Valdes.)
3 What did the Lord Deputy order Bingham to do with the Spaniards he had spared?
4 Why did Bingham spare the Dutchmen and boys?
5 What did the Lord Deputy have done with them?

A Spanish officer, Captain Francisco de Cuellar, describes his own shipwreck on the coast of Ireland:

Document Three
I went to the top deck of my ship, and, having prayed to God and Our Lady, looked at the terrible scene. Many were drowning in their ships; others jumped into the water and sank straight to the bottom; others were on rafts, or clinging to barrels and pieces of timber; others stood in their ships and called on God; others were swept from their ships by the waves. I stood looking at this dreadful sight, not knowing what to do. I could not swim and the waves and the storm were very great. Moreover, the beach was crowded with enemies who were jumping with joy at our misfortunes. As soon as any of our men reached land, two hundred savages fell upon him and stripped him naked. They then beat and wounded him without mercy. All this could be clearly seen from the damaged ships.
Francisco de Cuellar to a friend, 4 October, 1589

1 How were many of the Spaniards drowning?
2 How did some of them reach the shore?
3 What happened to them when they arrived?

De Cuellar managed to reach the shore by clinging to a hatch cover. He was injured and bleeding and, perhaps for that reason, he was not attacked. When he had recovered a little, he made his way inland.

Some of the native Irish had been carried away at the chance of plunder. However, they were Catholics and they hated the English. When he was safely away from the coast, de Cuellar found numbers of them who were willing to help him. After many adventures he made his way to Scotland, and from there to Flanders, where the Duke of Parma was.

De Cuellar was brave and intelligent, so he deserved to escape, but he was also very lucky. Almost all the Spaniards who landed in Ireland, died there.

J The English after the Fighting

After the defeat of the Armada, there were services of thanksgiving in churches all over England. The men in the fleet, though, had no cause to rejoice. Here are extracts from two of Howard's letters:

Document One

a. The sailors cry out for money and know not when they are to be paid. I have given them my word and honour that I will see them paid. If I had not done so, they would have run away from Plymouth by thousands.
Howard to Walsingham, 9 August, 1588

b. My Lords, I must warn you of great discontentments among the men here. They had hoped, after so good service, to have received their whole pay. Finding they have so little, it breeds a marvellous alteration among them.
Howard to the Council, 22 August, 1588

1 Why are the English sailors worried and discontented?

Here is another of Howard's letters:

Document Two

Sickness and death begin to wonderfully grow among us. It is a most pitiful sight to see, here at Margate, how the men, having no place to go, die in the streets. I myself have to come ashore to find them some lodging; and the best I can get is barns and outhouses; and the help is small that I can provide for them there. It would grieve any man's heart to see them that have served so bravely to die so miserably.
Howard to Burghley, 10 August, 1588

Note: The disease that was killing the men was, perhaps, typhus. It is unpleasant and deadly.

1 Where, in Margate, are sailors dying?

2 What are the only places Howard can find, for the sick men to go?

Howard's letter goes on:

Figure 1 The Armada Portrait of Queen Elizabeth Contrast this portrait of the Queen with the description of her sailors after the fighting.

Document Three
The *Elizabeth Jonas*, which hath done as well as any ship, hath had a great infection in her from the beginning. Of the 500 men that we carried out, by the time we had been in Plymouth a month, there were dead of them 200 and more.

It is likely that the infection will grow through most of our fleet; for our men have been so long at sea that they have little shift of apparel, and no money to buy it. Some have been – yea for the most part – these eight months at sea.
Howard to Burghley, 10 August, 1588

Note: 'shift of apparel' – change of clothes

1 How many men had there been in the *Elizabeth Jonas*? How many died?
2 Why have the men's clothes worn out? Why are they unable to buy more?

Some days later Howard wrote:

Document Four
The most part of the fleet is seriously infected. The men die daily, falling sick in great numbers; and the ships themselves are so infectious, and so corrupted, as it is thought to be a very plague. We find that the fresh men that we draw into our ships are infected one day and die the next. Many of the ships have hardly enough men to weigh their anchors.
Howard to the Council, 22 August, 1588

1 Imagine you are a sailor in the English fleet. Say how you feel about what happened after the defeat of the Armada.

K The Dutch and the Armada

As you saw in the Introduction, the Netherlands rebelled against Philip II in 1568. By 1588 the people of the northern provinces, that is the Dutch, had driven out the Spaniards. The Dutch had many good ships, so the English hoped they would help fight the Armada. But just after the Battle of Gravelines, Howard noted with disappointment, 'There is not one Hollander at sea.'

When the fighting was over, a member of the Dutch government wrote to the English Privy Council:

Document One
We praise and glorify God that it has pleased Him to give good success to her Majesty's navy against our common enemy. It was unfortunate that we could not support you to make the victory more complete. But the mutinies among our soldiers prevented us.

On the other hand, you will see how certain it is that the Duke of Parma will, in his fury, turn the great army he has gathered in Flanders against this country, to revenge the loss and shame his master has had at sea. We beg you to send us large numbers of soldiers, especially horsemen, of which we are very short.
Huygens to the Privy Council, August, 1588

1 Why were the Dutch unable to fight the Armada?
2 What do they fear Parma will do?
3 What do they ask the English to do?

In one way, though, the Dutch did give invaluable help. If the Spaniards were to invade England, then Parma would have to cross the Straits of Dover. All he had was flat bottomed river barges. The Armada could not go to Dunkirk to meet Parma, because its large ships would be wrecked on the sandbanks near the coast. Parma would have to come out to meet the Armada. But lurking near Dunkirk was a Dutch commander called Justin of Nassau. He had a fleet of fly-boats. They were small, but they were fast and well-armed. If Parma's barges had left Dunkirk, then the Dutch fly-boats would have attacked them at once. The result would have been a massacre of the Spanish troops. Parma had no intention of letting that happen.

Thanks to the Dutch, then, the Spaniards were quite unable to invade England.

There were many reasons for the defeat of the Spanish Armada, but the most important was that Philip II gave his commanders a plan that was bound to fail.

7 Privateers

A Introduction

After the defeat of the Armada, it was the English who took the offensive. They made a few raids on Spain itself. For example, they sacked Cadiz in 1596. But these expeditions were costly, which meant that the Queen could not afford many. Instead, she allowed anyone who wanted, to go hunting for Spanish merchant ships. This is known as 'privateering'. It cost the government nothing, while, if they were lucky, the privateers themselves made a lot of money.

Let us now imagine it is 1600. We will ask a London merchant, Thomas Watts, to tell us about privateering.

'What ships do privateers sail in?'

'Ordinary merchant ships, as a rule. They carry a few extra big guns, but there is no point in giving them a great many. We want to capture our prizes, not sink them! It is more important for a privateer to carry plenty of men.'

'What do the men gain from a voyage?'

'In the first place, they take pillage from any ship that is captured. Pillage is goods that are not part of the cargo. For example, the captain will take his rival's property and the best gun. The master will take the Spanish master's sea chest and the best cable.'

'What happens to the cargo?'

'No-one should touch that until the prize is brought home. Then it is divided into three. The ship's owners have a third. The men who fitted out the ship have a third. The crew has a third. But sometimes, when they take a ship, the men run wild and rob the cargo. We call this "breaking bulk" '.

'Who are the people that send out privateers?'

'The most important group is merchants

Figure 1 Drawing of a Gallizabra This was sent to England by an English spy.

like me. We have plenty of strong ships. But traders, farmers, country gentlemen, all invest money in privateers. A few of the great nobles, like the Earl of Cumberland, gather powerful fleets and go to sea themselves.'

'What ships do you hope to capture?'

'Best of all, would be to capture some of the King of Spain's treasure ships, laden with silver. But there is little hope of that. Much of the treasure comes to Spain in vessels called gallizabras. They sail so fast that no English ship can catch them. The rest of the silver comes in powerful convoys. Next best, would be to capture a Portuguese carrack bringing spices from the East Indies. But these carracks are monsters of 2000 tons, while the average privateer is only 300 tons.'

'What ships do you capture, then?'

'Most of them are not exciting at all. Often, we take little ships carrying grain. Often, we take fishing boats. Sometimes we capture a cargo of wine. But the most valuable goods come from America. They are such things as logwood, indigo, hides, cotton, ginger, cochineal, and even silver and pearls. What we take most, though, and what makes us most money, is sugar.'

'Who does the best from privateering?'

Figure 2 Privateers attack a Spanish Settlement

'Merchants and shipowners like me. For example, if I send a ship to trade with Italy, she will earn me a good profit from her trade alone. But I also tell her captain to look for prizes. If he can take one, that is a bonus.'

'What about noblemen, like the Earl of Cumberland?'

'They spend so much money on their fleets that they are lucky if they cover their expenses. Their only hope is to capture some of the Spanish treasure fleet, or a Portuguese carrack. But, as I have explained, that is nearly impossible.'

'Has it ever happened?'

'In 1592, Cumberland's ships were part of a fleet that captured a Portuguese carrack, the *Madre de Dios*. The spices and other goods she was carrying must have been worth £500,000. But when they reached Dartmouth, the sailors broke bulk. They ran off with three quarters of the cargo. Then, two years later, Cumberland had an amazing piece of good luck. He came upon the carrack, the *Cinco Chagas*.

'That should have made Cumberland's fortune!'

'It should have done, but it didn't.'

'What went wrong?'

'He sank her.'

1 Why do privateers need plenty of men, rather than many guns?

2 What is pillage? Who has it?

3 How is the cargo of a prize shared?

4 What is 'breaking bulk'?

5 Name some of the people who take part in privateering.

6 What would be the best prizes to capture? Why is this difficult?

7 Name some of the cargoes privateers do take.

8 Which people do best out of privateering?

B A Privateering Voyage

In the Introduction, you learnt a little about the Earl of Cumberland. He went privateering because he was heavily in debt. He could have paid his debts by cutting down his expenses. However, he thought that privateering would be quicker, it would be more exciting, and it would earn him some glory into the bargain.

Here you are going to read about a voyage Cumberland made to the Azores in 1589. The Azores is a group of islands, well out in the Atlantic. It belongs to Portugal. We know what happened on the voyage because one of Cumberland's men, Edward Wright, wrote an account of it.

The Queen lent Cumberland one of her best ships, the *Victory*, and he had three other vessels. He left Plymouth on June 18th. 1589. As you know, the richest prizes were the Portuguese carracks coming from the East Indies, and the Spanish treasure ships coming from America. Cumberland tried to capture some of both. This is what happened about the carracks:

Figure 1 The Earl of Cumberland Here, he is dressed as the Queen's Champion.

Document One

We were about Flores when a little English ship called the *Drake* brought us word that the carracks were at Terceira. At this news we were very glad, and sped that way with all the speed we could.

The Voyage of the Earl of Cumberland to the Azores

Note: Terceira is an island in the Azores.

1 What did the crew of the *Drake* tell Cumberland?

Later, Cumberland's men saw a strange sight:

Document Two

The last day of August we came in sight of Terceira, when we saw a small boat under sail, which seemed strange to us, being so far from land. But coming near, we found they were eight Englishmen that had been prisoners in Terceira. They had escaped, and put to sea, trusting in God. They had no other yard for their sail but two pipe staves tied together, and no more victuals than they could bring in their pockets. Having taken them all into the *Victory*, they gave us certain news that the carracks were departed from Terceira a week before.

The Voyage of the Earl of Cumberland to the Azores

Note: 'pipe staves' – curved boards used to make barrels

1 Whom did Cumberland's men rescue?
2 What news did they have?

This is what happened about the treasure fleet:

Document Three

When we were three or four leagues from Terceira, we saw fifteen sail of the West Indian fleet coming into the haven at Angra in

Figure 2 (above) Portuguese Carrack It was ships like these that Cumberland was hoping to capture.

Figure 3 Seville This was the port in Spain to which the treasure fleet sailed. The English never prevented it from arriving.

Terceira. We came very near the harbour mouth, being minded to have run in among them, and to have fetched out some of them, if it had been possible. But in the end, this was deemed too dangerous, considering the strength of the place where they rode. They were towed in near the town, lying under the protection of the Castle of Brasill on the one side (having in it five and twenty guns) and a fort on the other side wherein were thirteen or fourteen great brass cannon.
The Voyage of the Earl of Cumberland to the Azores

1 Where did Cumberland's men find the treasure fleet?
2 Why did they not attack it?

Cumberland was, however, luckier with other prizes:

Document Four

a. The first of August we had sight of the island of St. Michael, being one of the easternmost of the Azores. We sailed towards it, having put forth a Spanish flag so that they might not suspect us. We saw some ships riding at anchor, which we determined to take in the dark of night. About ten of the clock we sent our boats well manned to cut their cables and let them drive into the sea. Three small ships that lay near under the castle there, our men let loose and towed them away unto us. Most of the Spaniards that were in them leapt overboard, and swam to shore with loud and lamentable cries. These ships were loaded with wine and oil from Seville.

b. The seventh of August we had sight of a little ship which we chased with our pinnace (the weather being calm) and towards evening we overtook her. There were in her 30 tuns of Madeira wine, certain woollen cloth, silk, etc.

c. The sixth of November Captain Preston saw a sail two or three leagues ahead of us, after which we hastened our chase and overtook her. She came from Brazil laden with sugar and logwood. As soon as we had taken her, a man in the main top saw another sail ahead. So at once we pursued this new chase with all the sails we could pack on and overtook her. She had prepared to fight us, having hanged the sides of the ship so thick with hides that musket shot could not have pierced them. But as soon as we discharged two of our big guns at her, she struck sail. We asked where they came from and they answered, from the West Indies. This ship was of some three or four hundred tons, and had in her seven hundred hides worth ten shillings each, six chests of cochineal, every chest containing one hundred pound weight, and every pound worth twenty-six shillings and eight pence, and certain chests of sugar and china dishes, with some plate and silver.
The Voyage of the Earl of Cumberland to the Azores

Notes: 'logwood' – material for making dye
'tun' – barrel holding 150 gallons

1 Where had each of the prizes come from?
2 What goods were they carrying?
3 Show this information in a table with the two headings:
Country of Origin; Cargo.

We will now look at the discipline in Cumberland's fleet. Here is what happened when his men took the town of Fayal:

Document Five

My Lord commanded that no sailor or soldier should enter any house to plunder it. But especially he was careful that the churches and monasteries should not be touched, which was done through his mounting guards on those places. But the rest of the town was ransacked by the soldiers and sailors, who scarcely left any house unsearched. They took such things as chests, chairs, cloth, coverlets, hangings, bedding, clothing; and further ranged into the country, where some of them were hurt by the inhabitants.
The Voyage of the Earl of Cumberland to the Azores

1 What orders did Cumberland give?
2 Which buildings was Cumberland able to protect?
3 What happened to the rest of the town?

From time to time the fleet ran out of water, and they had difficulty in finding more. Here

Figure 4 One of Queen Elizabeth's ships Cumberland's flagship was a vessel like this.

is what happened towards the end of October:

Document Six

On Monday October 27th we came to St. George's Island, where we espied a spout of water running down. The pinnace and the longboat were at once manned and sent under Captain Preston and Captain Munson.

And on Wednesday following, our boats returned with fresh water, whereof they brought only six tuns for the *Victory*, pretending they could get no more. They thought that since my Lord had only 12 tuns of water and wine, he would not go for the coast of Spain, but straight to England, as many of our men desired greatly. None the less, my Lord was unwilling to do so, and wanted the next day to take in more water. But through the unwillingness of his men, it was not done. Yet my Lord did not wish to return without taking enough prizes to make a profit from the voyage.

The Voyage of the Earl of Cumberland to the Azores

1 How much water did the boats fetch?
2 Many of the men wanted the fleet to be short of water. What did they hope this would force Cumberland to do?
3 Why was Cumberland unwilling to do this?

This is how the problem was solved:

Document Seven

Because no more water could now be gotten, the matter was referred to the choice of the whole company, whether they should tarry longer, till we might find enough fresh water, or go by the coast of Spain for England, with half as much allowance of drink as before. They willingly agreed that every mess should be allowed at one meal but half as much drink as usual, and so go for England, taking the coast of Spain in our way, to see if we could that way make up our voyage.

The Voyage of the Earl of Cumberland to the Azores

Note: 'make up our voyage' – take enough prizes to make a profit

You can see that Cumberland did not have enough authority to say what should be done. He had to ask his men.

1 What did they agree to do about the shortage of water?
2 Which route home did they agree to take?
3 What did they hope to do on the way?

Cumberland managed to capture several good prizes off the coast of Spain. Edward

Figure 5 Dutch East Indiaman, early seventeenth century

Wright wrote, 'And now we had our hands full, and with joy shaped our course for England.' All might have been well, but the fleet ran into head winds and a heavy storm. The winds kept them at sea for several weeks and, since they were short of water, many men died of thirst. Also, the storm wrecked their best prize on the coast of Cornwall.

Cumberland did make a profit from this voyage, but it was only a modest one. He went on several other voyages, some of which were complete failures. Taking them all into account, he lost money. In the end, he gave up privateering. He was more heavily in debt than when he had started.

We must now see what happened in the privateering war as a whole.

Unlike Cumberland, many men did make good profits. As you saw in the Introduction, they were, for the most part, merchants. They did well because they were careful not to spend too much money fitting out their ships. Also, they knew who would give them the best prices for the goods they had captured. However, though we cannot be sure, they would probably have made just as much money if they had been able to trade peacefully with Spain.

As for the Spaniards and the Portuguese, they lost only three carracks. They were the two you read about and another, the *San Felipe*. Not a single ship from the American treasure fleet was lost to the English. However, the Spaniards used so many of their warships to bring home the treasure that there were none left to look after the ordinary merchant ships. The privateers took a great many of these and when the war ended in 1604, the Spaniards and the Portuguese did not have nearly enough to carry all their goods. That meant they had to pay the merchants of other countries to do this for them. Here was a splendid opportunity for the English to make a lot of money, but they did not seize it. Instead, the Dutch took the trade. They had better ships, and they were better business men.